HOW TO SORT YOUR HEAD OUT

Build your Self-Esteem by Understanding Your Emotional Fears

Copyright © 2017 by Luke Pemberton

All rights reserved. No part of this publication may be reproduced, distributed or transmitted in any form or by any means, including photocopying, recording, or other electronic or mechanical methods, without the prior written permission of the publisher, except in the case of brief quotations embodied in critical reviews and certain other noncommercial uses permitted by copyright law.

Published by: Luke Pemberton

ISBN: 978-1981701957

TABLE OF CONTENTS

Introduction 9

Part 1: Understanding things further to fully save yourself 11

    This is me now 12

    It's got a lot to do with your childhood and parents (probably), continued… 18

    Attach to the 'mother ship' or drift in deep space – attachment theory 19

    What didn't happen to you can be the problem – childhood emotional neglect 28

    Giving up your childhood – maternal enmeshment and co-dependency 32

    Killing your own soul – the effects of toxic shame contamination 42

    Shamed, fearful children are ripe for religious indoctrination 56

    Thoughts that scare you – obsessive-compulsive disorder 59

    Lost and scared in an impossible emotional maze 65

    How these emotional experiences manifested themselves in adulthood 76

    A permanent state of mental exhaustion 80

    Excruciating insecurity, paranoid thoughts 84

    Subconsciously looking for a surrogate mother and father 90

Grooves, DEFCON and Angry Birds 95

Understanding the implications – Inner Family Therapy 98

Part 2: Saving yourself 101

Challenging your assumptions and facing your fears 104

Black is white and vice versa 107

Overcoming wrongful (emotional) conviction.................... 108

A brief pep talk 113

Overcoming toxic shame 116

Be wary – falling into burnout and depression 122

Alcohol – so very tempting 131

My time in a recovery clinic 135

Managing your recovery process 138

Improving the way you think – mental models 145

The power of imagination – utilise it to the full! 148

Managing the process – some more tips 151

A. **Conclusion** 157
B. **Appendices** 159

ABOUT THE AUTHOR

LUKE PEMBERTON most recently worked in the political department of a large international organisation dealing with the prevention of international conflict and post-conflict crisis management. This is his second book.

To my nephew and friend Tom, and to Rasa O

INTRODUCTION

Writing my first book *How to Find the Way Out When in Despair* was a cathartic experience for me. It helped me hugely to overcome my demons, all those irrational but deeply felt fears and insecurities that had been roaming around in my subconscious mind for decades, occasionally springing into my consciousness to cause me acute anxiety and insecurity on a daily if not hourly, basis. I very much hope the book helped others to realise they are not alone in their suffering. However, I realised after finishing the book that there was still an awful lot of negative stuff floating around inside me which I needed to expunge, before I could really behave like a 'normal' person unencumbered by latent and frankly nonsensical fears from years gone by. As a result, I decided to write this follow-up account to explain to myself what it was that continued to disorientate me and upset my psychological and emotional well-being.

As with the first book, I have attempted to be brutally honest in describing my fears and insecurities, and how I addressed them, to paint as authentic a picture as possible of the inner workings of my mind. Some of the issues covered in the first book are looked at again here, but from different angles.

The structure of the book is also broadly similar: a brief update on my emotional status; a review of my personal story in order to try and understand what can drive a person's debilitating insecurities and fears; how these can manifest themselves in adulthood; more tools on how we can understand what is going on inside us; an overview of how I overcame these issues; a word on burnout, depression, and alcohol; and finally, some additional tips on managing your return to secure emotional well-being.

As I've said, I very much hope that, after reading my account, those who are experiencing, or have experienced, similar feelings of self-doubt and low self-esteem will realise that they are not alone in their feelings. One of my worst experiences was the belief that only I had such extreme self-doubt, negative feelings and disturbing images flying around my mind on a regular basis. Knowing you are not alone in this respect is very comforting and reassuring. To my mind, the need to realise there are many of us struggling out there is critical.

I would like again to state from the outset that this book is not meant to be a criticism of my parents in any way as they themselves seem to have experienced difficult and turbulent emotional periods earlier in their lives (and indeed subsequently).

PART 1

UNDERSTANDING THINGS FURTHER TO FULLY SAVE YOURSELF

THIS IS ME NOW.

Still happily married with a lovely family

(and even a shrinking beer belly)

This is me, writing my follow-up book

I wrote my first book as I was facing a self-esteem crisis in my life.

UNDERSTANDING THINGS FURTHER TO FULLY SAVE YOURSELF 13

> LUKE PEMBERTON
> How to find the Way Out when in despair

At the time, my self-esteem was as small as a tiny shed compared to that of 'normal' people, whose self-esteem seemed to me to be as huge as London skyscraper the Shard.

> THE LONDON SHARD
> BIG TOWER! ↑
>
> IF THE LONDON SHARD REPRESENTS 'NORMAL' PEOPLE'S SELF-ESTEEM, MY MINI-SHED BELOW REPRESENTS MY SELF-ESTEEM BEFORE WRITING MY FIRST BOOK
>
> ME, AND MY TINY GARDEN SHED

Despite writing the first book, I still felt after its publication that there was a lot of emotional pain and fear within me that was almost bursting to come out.

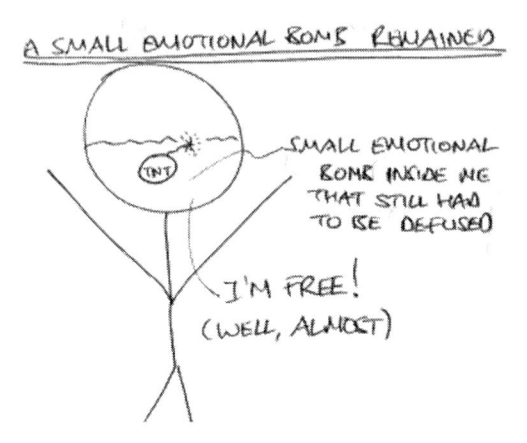

A SMALL EMOTIONAL BOMB REMAINED

SMALL EMOTIONAL BOMB INSIDE ME THAT STILL HAD TO BE DEFUSED

I'M FREE! (WELL, ALMOST)

This ticking emotional bomb felt like a volcano of emotions inside me.

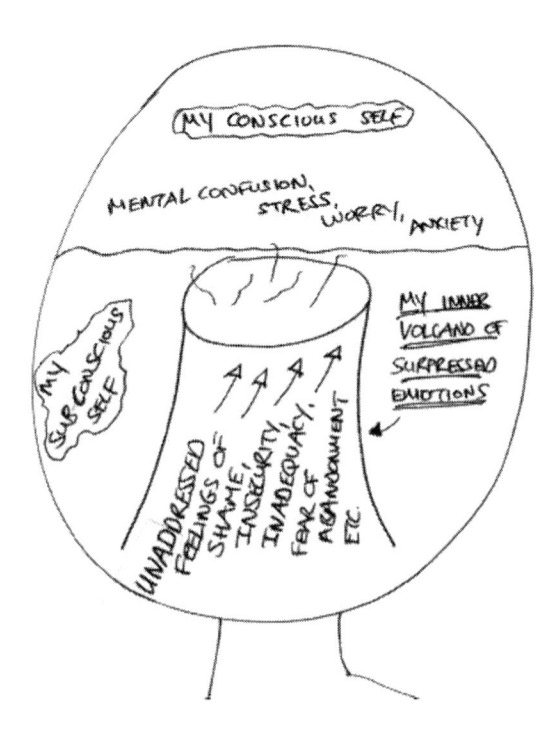

MY CONSCIOUS SELF

MENTAL CONFUSION, STRESS, WORRY, ANXIETY

MY SUBCONSCIOUS SELF

MY INNER VOLCANO OF SUPPRESSED EMOTIONS

UNADDRESSED FEELINGS OF SHAME, INSECURITY, INADEQUACY, FEAR OF ABANDONMENT ETC.

All this was having a detrimental physical and mental effect on me and would have caused me (and my family by association) significant distress if not addressed.

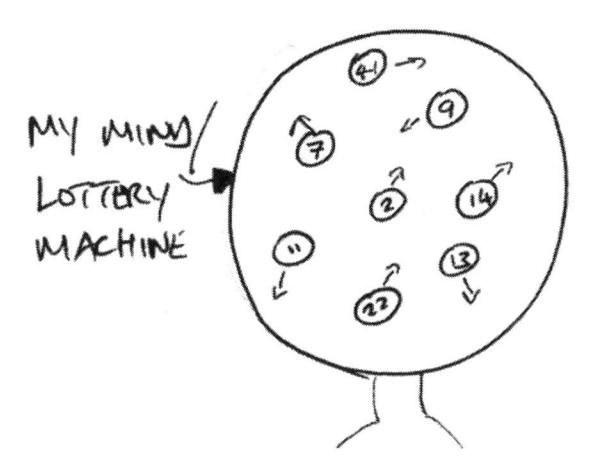

[Sketch: a head labeled "MY MIND/LOTTERY MACHINE" containing numbered balls (4, 7, 9, 2, 14, 11, 13, 22) with arrows showing them bouncing around.]

My thoughts felt like ping-pong balls flying around in a lottery machine, rarely stopping despite my efforts to calm them down.

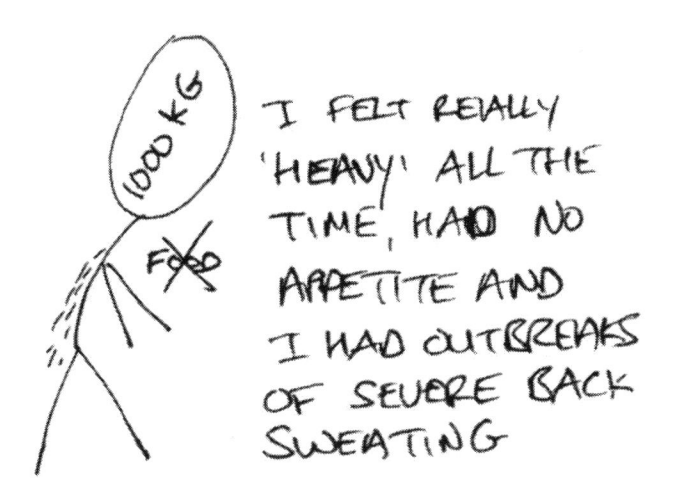

[Sketch: a stick figure with a large head labeled "1000 KG" and crossed-out "FOOD", with text:] I FELT REALLY 'HEAVY' ALL THE TIME, HAD NO APPETITE AND I HAD OUTBREAKS OF SEVERE BACK SWEATING

I also had sudden periods of extreme gum ache, gnashing and grinding of teeth at night, violent and aggressive thoughts, and at times a frightening inability to control my thinking. In general, I felt rather shell shocked.

Worst of all, I felt mentally wiped out.

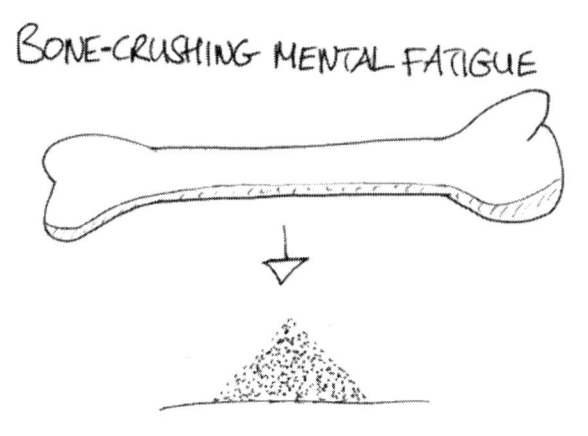

BONE-CRUSHING MENTAL FATIGUE

After a few years of taking intermittent sick leave, I realised something had to give. To ensure I could sort myself out once and for all, I very reluctantly resigned from my job, which I had felt really privileged to have with the hope that writing about the remaining emotional turbulence within me could help achieve this goal.

This is me leaving my work building, which had a lovely and rewarding working environment, for the last time.

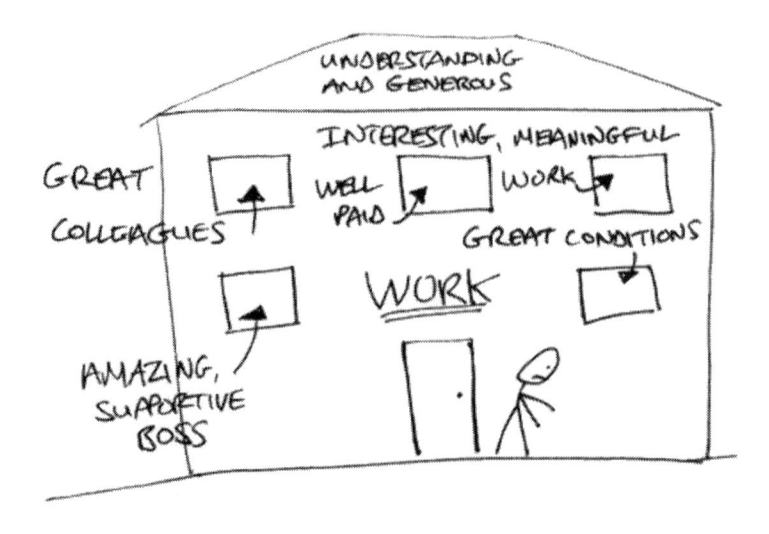

UNDERSTANDING AND GENEROUS · INTERESTING, MEANINGFUL WORK · GREAT COLLEAGUES · WELL PAID · GREAT CONDITIONS · AMAZING, SUPPORTIVE BOSS · WORK

After a bit of rest, I wrote this book to vent the volcano and defuse the bomb.

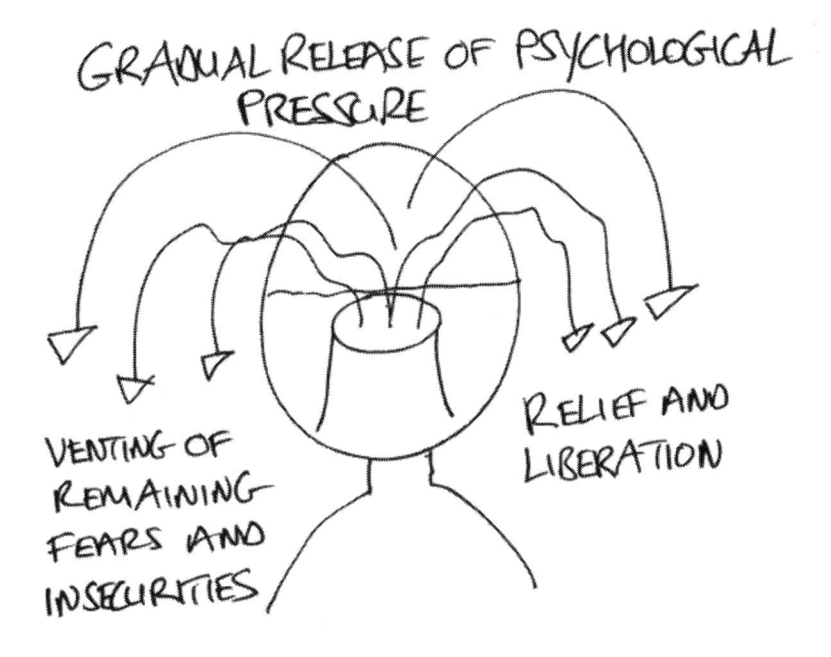

IT'S GOT A LOT TO DO WITH YOUR CHILDHOOD AND PARENTS (PROBABLY), CONTINUED...

In my first book, I mentioned the likelihood that any emotional fears and insecurities most people feel are perhaps linked to their experiences as children with their parents or other primary care givers. (References to parents throughout include primary caregivers.) Once I had time to consider my emotions again, the first thing I did was to review my childhood experiences.

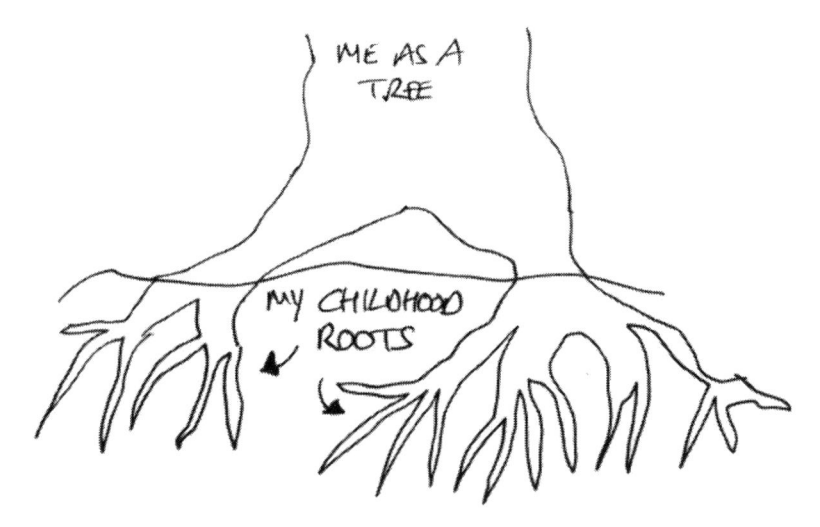

ME AS A TREE

MY CHILDHOOD ROOTS

And that brought me to the topic of attachment theory.

ATTACH TO THE 'MOTHER SHIP' OR DRIFT IN DEEP SPACE – ATTACHMENT THEORY

The basic premise of attachment theory (www.simplypsychology.org/attachment.html) is that we have a primeval, basic need to bond emotionally and securely with other humans and to feel that we belong and are safe to be ourselves without fear of retribution. According to John Bowlby, the British psychologist who developed these theories, successful emotional attachments depend on the type and quality of our earliest experiences with our parents.

According to Bowlby, children who have broadly positive emotional experiences with their parents enjoy secure attachment; those who experience insensitive interaction and/or emotional rejection from their parents generally develop insecure-avoidant attachment; those experiencing insensitive and/or inconsistent interaction generally become insecure-resistant; and those with more serious abusive experiences develop disorganised attachment. Of course, people may fit into more than one of these categories.

Secure attachment.

Broadly speaking, this attachment experience results in an emotionally secure adult who feels confident in their self-worth.

Anxious-ambivalent (or anxious-preoccupied) attachment.

Here the child is anxious when the mother, for example, is suddenly absent, then becomes ambivalent about her presence when she returns. This form of early attachment relationship can lead to relationship difficulties in adults. According to the Wikipedia entry on attachment in adults, such people tend to agree with the statement, "I am uncomfortable being without close relationships, but I sometimes worry that others don't value me as much as I value them". They tend to sometimes be clingy, jealous, coercive, and angry with lots of childhood existential angst and fear – they feel the relationship could end at any time.

Anxious-avoidant (or dismissive-avoidant) attachment.

These experiences often result in the child as an adult having a defensive view towards relationships, trying to avoid them out of fear of being hurt or rejected again, and digging up all their childhood fears. Such people also often dismiss the need for intimate relationships (often unwittingly and disingenuously).

Disorganised/disoriented (or fearful-avoidant) attachment.

VERY PROBLEMATIC CHILDHOODS ⇨ DISORGANISED or FEARFUL-AVOIDANT ADULTS

People in this category often have very negative views about their own self-worth and are sometimes scared of the emotional intentions of others. All this seems to make logical sense with hindsight, but it was a rather ground-breaking theory to begin with. When I came across it, the notion and sense of insecure attachment with a parent(s) rang a few bells for me. Diane Benoit, professor of psychiatry at the University of Toronto, confirms the importance of a parent's role as an attachment figure (www.ncbi.nlm.nih.gov/pmc/articles/PMC2724160/):

> Parents play many distinct roles in the lives of their children, including teacher, playmate, disciplinarian, caregiver and attachment figure. Of all these roles, their role as an attachment figure is one of the most important in predicting the child's later social and emotional outcome… Attachment is a powerful predictor of a child's later social and emotional outcome… Attachment is where the child uses the primary caregiver as a secure base from which to explore and, when necessary, as a haven of safety and a source of comfort secure, insecure-avoidant, insecure-resistant and insecure-disorganized.

After inquiring a bit more about my own childhood, it seems I often sought assurance as an infant and was regarded as a sensitive child.

I realised later in life that I was sometimes left alone as an infant for periods that were perhaps too prolonged.

It should of course be noted that insecure attachment often happens because the parents themselves experienced attachment problems when they were children and their emotional insecurity is unwittingly passed on to their children.

I was a huge fan of the film *The Black Hole*, and of course the *Star Wars* trilogy, as a kid. It is against this backdrop that I now see my childhood experience of attachment.

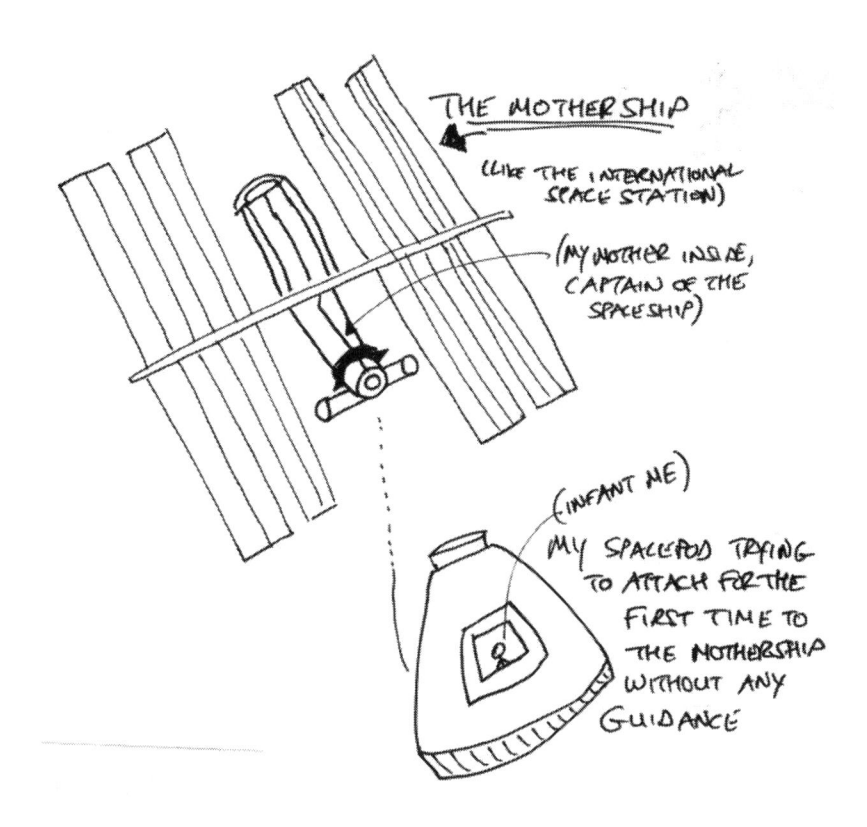

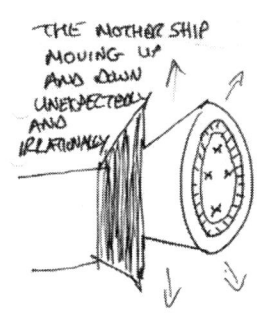

UNDERSTANDING THINGS FURTHER TO FULLY SAVE YOURSELF   23

24 How to Sort Your Head Out

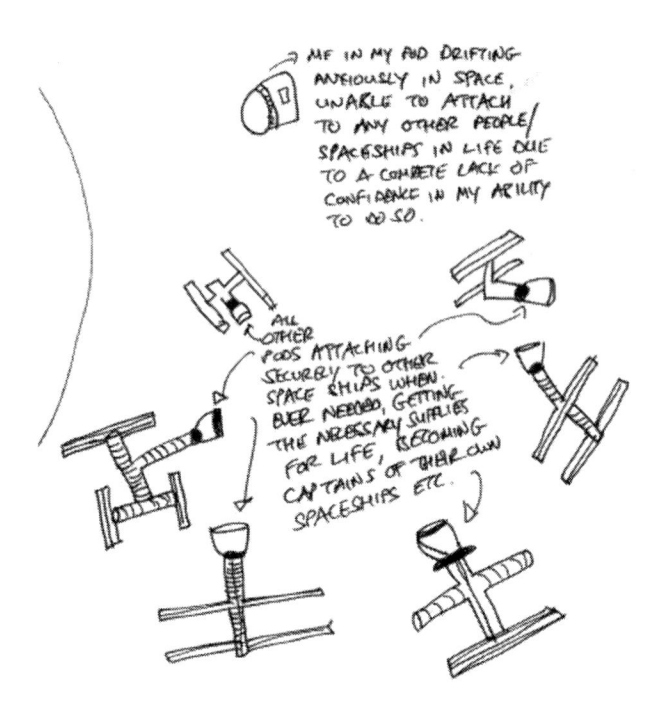

Another image that springs to my mind to describe how I failed to attach emotionally early in life is the following:

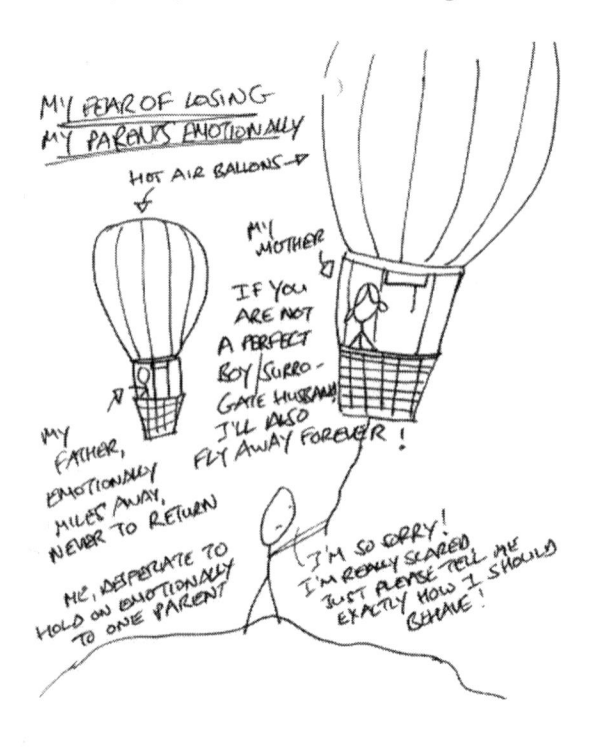

Insecure attachment also applies of course to a child's relationship with its father. My father was a busy man and sometimes I felt he didn't have time for me. (I guess this may have been the case for many of us). I have a sense that this was a contributing factor to my developing a stutter when I was young, and a subsequent tendency to talk very quickly out of a fear of losing the attention of the listener.

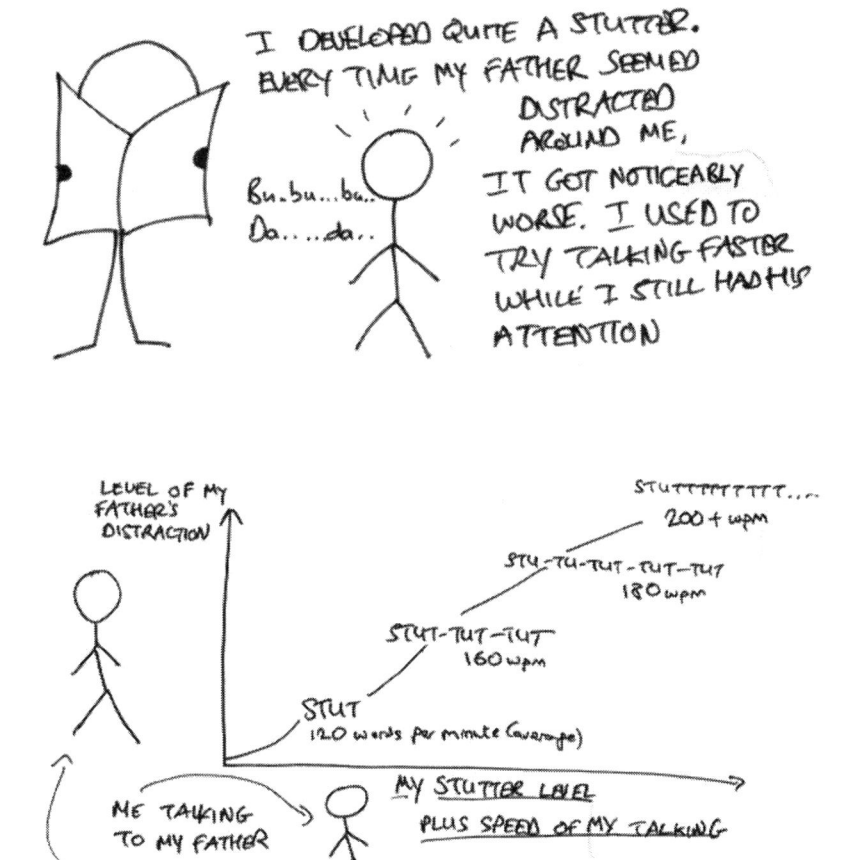

Bu..bu...bu..
Da......da..

I DEVELOPED QUITE A STUTTER. EVERY TIME MY FATHER SEEMED DISTRACTED AROUND ME, IT GOT NOTICEABLY WORSE. I USED TO TRY TALKING FASTER WHILE I STILL HAD HIS ATTENTION

LEVEL OF MY FATHER'S DISTRACTION

STUTTTTTTTTT... 200+ wpm
STU-TU-TUT-TUT-TUT 180 wpm
STUT-TUT-TUT 160 wpm
STUT 120 words per minute (average)

ME TALKING TO MY FATHER

MY STUTTER LEVEL PLUS SPEED OF MY TALKING

Elaborating on this subject of male attachment, many of us who have had similar experiences may also have felt as I did, that I never measured up to my father's expectations and, as a result, to other boys in our social circle.

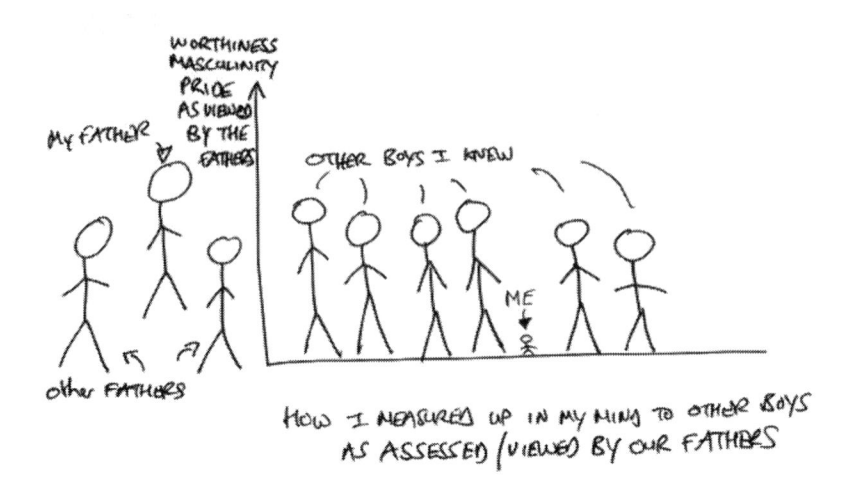

[Figure: A hand-drawn diagram with stick figures. At left, a tall figure labeled "MY FATHER" stands next to a bar reaching up to "WORTHINESS MASCULINITY PRIDE AS VIEWED BY THE FATHERS". Smaller figures below are labeled "other FATHERS". To the right, a row of stick figures labeled "OTHER BOYS I KNEW" with one very small figure labeled "ME". Caption: "HOW I MEASURED UP IN MY MIND TO OTHER BOYS AS ASSESSED/VIEWED BY OUR FATHERS"]

I remember one moment when I felt so small and ashamed. My father and I were playing a father-son golf competition. The other son holed a long putt and hugged his father in celebration. I missed a shorter putt and I remember my father turning his back on me and walking away. I'm sure this was not malicious in any way, but it was a culmination of many experiences which left me convinced I had let him down beyond measure.

[Figure: Hand-drawn stick-figure scene titled "ONCE I MISSED A PUTT WHEN PLAYING GOLF WITH MY FATHER". Labels: "MY FATHER WALKING AWAY, TO MY MIND IN TOTAL EMBARRASSMENT AND DISAPPOINTMENT"; "ME MISSING A PUTT"; "THE OTHER FATHER AND SON TEAM CONGRATULATING EACH OTHER"; "I FELT CRUSHED AND TOTALLY DESPONDENT AND FILLED WITH DEEP SHAME. THAT MOMENT STILL HAUNTS ME TO THIS DAY"]

On the rare occasion he intervened in my life, I would often find it traumatic and upsetting for no obvious reason.

On the rare occasion my father intervened in my life, I would often find it very traumatic and upsetting, for no visible reason

"Do your homework!" — my father / me crying

Even now, when I'm alone in the same room as my father, I have the urge to flee due to feelings of acute anxiety

"Got to leave" — me / my father

We also had in our family a relative who was well-known among people interested in certain parts of 19th-century history. Having this 'famous' great-grandfather, whom I was named after, became a burden to me rather than an inspiration.

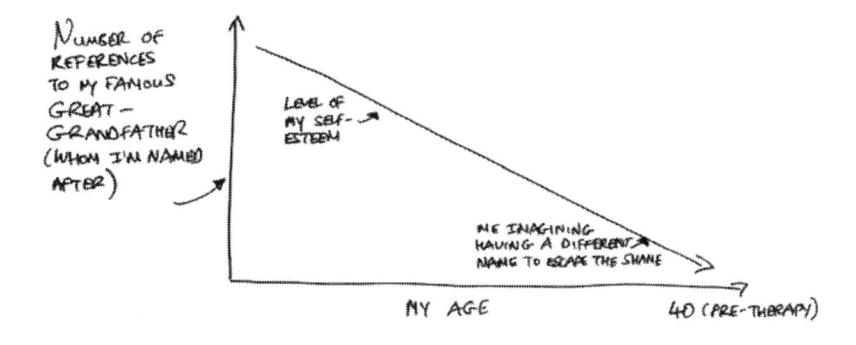

Number of references to my famous great-grandfather (whom I'm named after) / Level of my self-esteem / Me imagining having a different name to escape the shame / My age / 40 (pre-therapy)

WHAT *DIDN'T* HAPPEN TO YOU CAN BE THE PROBLEM – CHILDHOOD EMOTIONAL NEGLECT

This concept seemed counter-intuitive to me when I first considered it, but I'm sure there are many of us who could associate with it after some reflection. I assumed that something specific must have happened to me for me to feel so negatively about myself. This became maddening as I just couldn't put my finger on it.

It's driving me bananas!

Something must have happened to me. Some specific, traumatic event, but I can't for the life of me figure out what!

After a bit of research, I realised that often it's not what happened to people like us, but what *didn't* happen that's the problem. This could be an absence of praise, a dearth of tenderness, a lack of emotional warmth, too little respect and attention received, not being listened to or taken seriously, or simply a parent(s) not being around enough during formative years. This suddenly made a lot of sense to me and seemed to ring a few bells. Emotional withdrawal, emotional disengagement etc can be profoundly damaging for a child; the fear of not being seen, not being acknowledged, seemingly forgotten about, with nobody apparently wishing to connect with you. This can cause deep anxiety within a child, leading to the worst fear of all – that you are not worthy of being loved – and the rejection of your innate love for others as a child.

This malign neglect over many years can really knock your confidence.

My Shrinking Confidence

- "Here I am! Aren't I lovely! I'm so ready to love you both so much!" — My father playing golf. My mother castigating my sister!!

- "Hello!? It's me again... Ok, perhaps not so amazing but great nevertheless?" — My father, no response. "Luke, sometimes you drive me to despair!"

- "Uh, ok. Maybe I'm just about bearable though?" — My father, gone... "Gosh, life is so difficult for me at the moment"

- "Uh, ok... Not even bearable it seems. I'm the cause of their disinterest and suffering. My poor parents, I'm so sorry!" — My father still gone. "Please go away, I can't deal with you now..."

- "I really hate myself for annoying them and hurting them so much. I'm such an idiot and a huge burden" — My father, still gone. "Oh good, Luke has gone to play on his own for a bit. Cup of tea time"

This passive and benign neglect, plus my mother's devotion towards her youngest child (my younger brother), led me to feel rather emotionally abandoned.

Understanding Things Further to Fully Save Yourself

I have tried to convey this sense of emotional abandonment in the drawing below.

I felt as a child that my parents had sped off without me, distracted by their own personal issues in life, leaving me emotionally stranded in a lifeboat.

GIVING UP YOUR CHILDHOOD – MATERNAL ENMESHMENT AND CO-DEPENDENCY

I covered this topic in an elementary fashion in my first book as I felt this occurred to me to a greater or lesser extent. I stated that, "My mother also used me for emotional support when I was very young. This was very confusing to say the least. This is known as maternal enmeshment." I also referred to her apparent request for me to be her 'surrogate husband', to provide her with emotional sustenance. I would like to develop these topics a bit further here. I was always very worried about upsetting my mother or disappointing her in any way, a sense that I'm sure others can no doubt relate to.

I was always desperately trying to make sure she was OK.

My head was like an emotional radio, always trying to tune into my mother's emotional needs, out of a deep fear of being condemned for not supporting her enough emotionally.

Understanding things further to fully save yourself   33

OTHER KIDS PLAYING FOOTBALL, ME FOCUSING ON MY MOTHER

Maternal enmeshment is also referred to as an emotionally incestuous mother–son relationship. Blogger 'Chase Townsend' describes such a parent (http://narcissismschild.com/2015/03/16/the-consequences-of-enmeshment/) as one who "expects her child to continually anticipate and meet her needs. In this role reversal, the child finds himself catering to his parent's physical and emotional needs. Meanwhile his needs go unmet." This partly occurred perhaps because of some difficult experiences of my mother's as a child and her possible desire as a lonely young mother to keep me close emotionally. However, regardless of probable causes, such behaviour can be very damaging for the child in question.

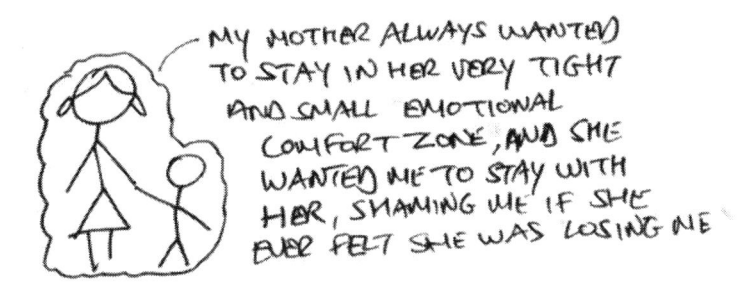

MY MOTHER ALWAYS WANTED TO STAY IN HER VERY TIGHT AND SMALL EMOTIONAL COMFORT ZONE, AND SHE WANTED ME TO STAY WITH HER, SHAMING ME IF SHE EVER FELT SHE WAS LOSING ME

In *Maternal Enmeshment, The Chosen Child* (journals.sagepub.com), Dr Dee Hann-Morrison states:

> Bradshaw (1989) termed this unhealthy bond spousification of the child, and characterized it as a blatant violation of the intimacy taboo between parent and child. The mother, in this and related cases, is preying on the child's admiration and unconditional love to meet a need for which children are

inadequately equipped—marital partnership…Ultimately, this child will stagnate in his emotional, as well as his social, development and will tend to function primarily in reaction to others… According to Love (1990), chosen child grows up being unsure of what is acceptable or peer appropriate behaviours and what isn't. In addition, as said by Love, as an adult, the victim of maternal enmeshment tends to be perfectionistic, and has a compulsive need to succeed. He will overcompensate in his efforts to appear at least normal…For the chosen child, emancipation requires GREAT EFFORT [her emphasis]—often more effort than this person is willing to invest, or can muster.…Growth from this arrested place of social and emotional stagnation requires the victim of maternal enmeshment to challenge long-held and deeply ingrained beliefs, not only about himself but also more importantly about the system from which he comes.

Lego blocks.

Everyone needs emotional security which gives them the Lego blocks in their lives to build their own emotional defences behind which they can retreat when feeling vulnerable or beleaguered. I felt as if my mother took some of my Lego building blocks away from me as a child for her own use, before I had a chance to use them to build my own defences.

The drawing below depicts Lego building blocks that one needs to build one's own character.

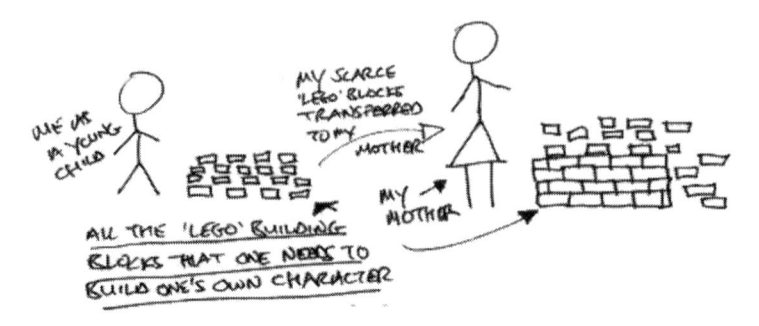

These blocks include pride, dignity, self-respect, confidence, love for self etc. Rather than rebuilding her own character deficiencies and insecurities with her own Lego blocks, or sourcing new ones from appropriate places, she took mine as it was easier (a subconscious decision driven by her own difficult childhood experiences).

This, combined with other factors, resulted in my having very weak defences. I was therefore very vulnerable to any form of criticism, no matter how slight it was, as I simply did not have the confidence in myself nor the experience of defending myself emotionally (which children learn is their right in emotionally healthier environments), a common weakness for many of us no doubt. (Feeling vulnerable on occasion per se is no bad thing of course; for more on this look at the famous TED talk on vulnerability by Brené Brown or go to www.brenebrown.com)

Emotionally healthy children or teenagers tend to be made of sturdy emotional bricks, each one added by a positive emotional experience as a child. These provide a reasonably good defence for everyday life and a sturdy enough place to retreat inside to when feeling emotionally vulnerable.

In contrast, I felt the everyday emotional winds blowing straight into me, with no real protection from the outside world. I also felt as if I had nowhere to retreat to when I felt emotionally vulnerable.

Because my father was emotionally and often physically distant, it meant I was rather trapped with my mother as my only caregiver – my grandparents, aunts and uncles lived some distance away – which exacerbated the situation.

Trapped in a distorted relationship with only one caregiver

Unfortunately, there was no other adult family member in the vicinity for me to turn to for emotional support. In addition, an emotional barrier existed between myself and my father. This lack of alternative outlet for my fears and frustrations led to a sense of helplessness and frustration, compounded by a sense of humiliation at not having the ego or ability to escape from a relationship I subconsciously realised was harming me.

I remember one instance when my mother's reaction to a simple event caused me real emotional confusion when I was about thirteen years old.

ONE DAY A FRIEND FROM SCHOOL CALLED ME AND SHE WAS CLEARLY OFFENDED THAT I WANTED TO SPEAK TO HIM, ACTING AS IF I HAD EMOTIONALLY BETRAYED HER.

This is one example of how I came to worry about my mother's well-being to the detriment of my own.

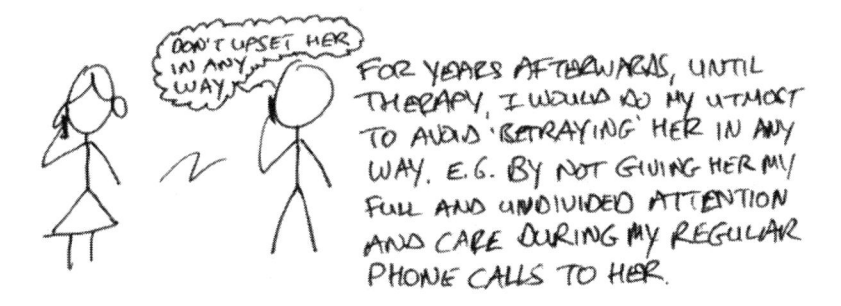

FOR YEARS AFTERWARDS, UNTIL THERAPY, I WOULD DO MY UTMOST TO AVOID 'BETRAYING' HER IN ANY WAY. E.G. BY NOT GIVING HER MY FULL AND UNDIVIDED ATTENTION AND CARE DURING MY REGULAR PHONE CALLS TO HER.

Being emotionally trapped with a primary caregiver can lead to real confusion on the part of the child, who often makes many fixed assumptions because of the experience.

Emotional incest/relational trauma.

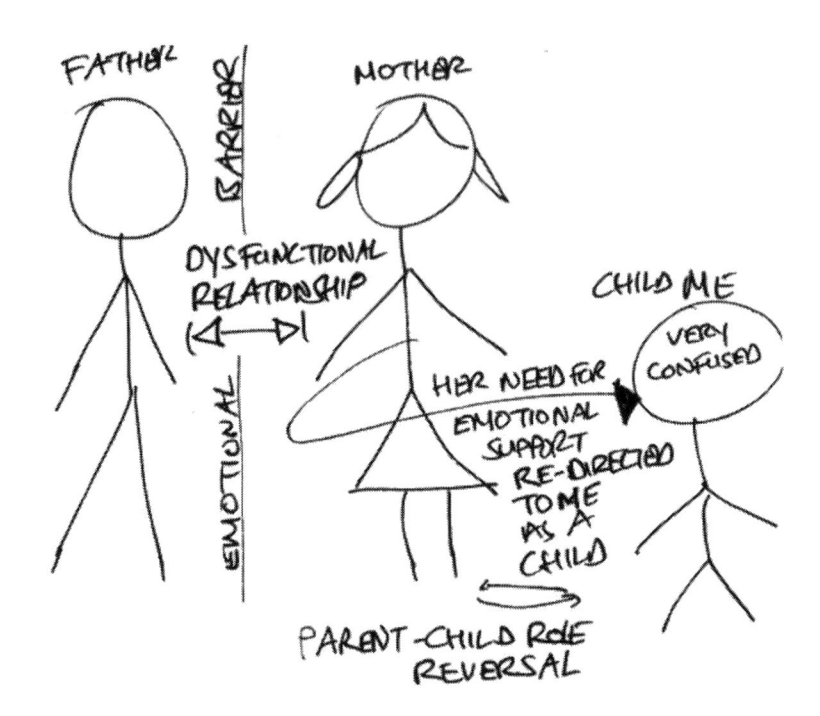

[Diagram: Stick figures labeled FATHER and MOTHER with a "BARRIER" between them. Annotations: "DYSFUNCTIONAL RELATIONSHIP ⟷", "EMOTIONAL" (vertical), "HER NEED FOR EMOTIONAL SUPPORT RE-DIRECTED TO ME AS A CHILD" pointing to a smaller stick figure labeled "CHILD ME / VERY CONFUSED". Below: "PARENT-CHILD ROLE REVERSAL".]

My take away messages or beliefs from the situation depicted above included: Other people's emotional needs are more important than mine; I am a resource for other people to use as they please; the person involved will always return to their preferred other person, and I will be used by others afterwards; I am an 'object' with no inherent self-worth; and I have no trust in myself to attract love or in others to provide it. As a result, I had no understanding of real emotional security.

Co-dependency and maternal enmeshment.

According to Shawn M. Burn, in www.psychologytoday.com/blog/presence-mind/201307/are-you-in-codependent-relationship:

> [In adult terms] co-dependent relationships are close re-lationships where much of the love and intimacy in the

relationship is experienced in the context of one person's distress and the other's rescuing or enabling. The helper shows love primarily through the provision of assistance and the other feels loved primarily when they receive assistance. In the co-dependent relationship, the helper's emotional enmeshment leads them to keenly feel the other's struggles and to feel guilt at the thought of limiting their help…These helpers are often dependent on the other's poor functioning to satisfy emotional needs such as the need to feel needed, and the need to keep the other close due to fears of abandonment. Feeling competent (relative to the other) also boosts the low self-esteem of some helpers.

When this applies to a mother's relationship to her son, the effects on the child can be very serious. In this context, I note an interesting article by Lana Blackmore on this topic at https://wehavekids.com/family-relationships/8-Signs-You-May-Have-a-Codependent-Parent:

Having a co-dependent mother, paradoxically means the mother seems to have all the control, but she needs the child almost more than the child needs her as a companion. She may deep down be isolated and lonely with a victim mentality, too weak or scared or ill-resourced to confront her own problems, wanting and believing that others should do it for her. Rather than dealing with the traumas and difficulties in their own life through healthy means such as self-reflection and therapy, the co-dependent parent latches onto a child and demands compensation. … the Co-dependent Parent Also Manipulates – Subtly; … The most effective form of manipulation is the kind that you can never be called out for directly. Examples include the silent treatment, passive aggressive comments, denial of wrongdoing and projection, among others. The co-dependent parent will leave the child in a state of confusion, wondering who really is "the bad guy"…Often, the parents will be genuinely unaware of their own manipulation.

As far as I can tell, I also reacted to my mother's unintended emotional manipulation of me in a co-dependent manner. I gladly took on this role of a shoulder to cry on and this in turn encouraged my mother to use me further in such a function (more prevalent among the males of us, I gather, although the females of us of course suffer equally in different ways). This affected me in diverse ways growing up. I remember once desperately trying to be the perfect son, like a puppy dog desperate for its owner's approval, during a day trip to London, while my brother acted like a normal boy.

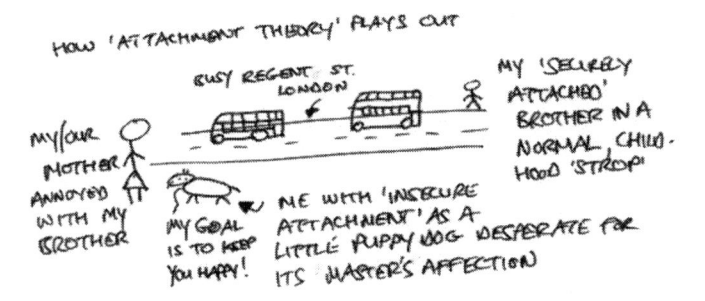

[Hand-drawn illustration: "HOW 'ATTACHMENT THEORY' PLAYS OUT" — showing a busy Regent St. London scene with buses, mother annoyed with brother, "MY GOAL IS TO KEEP YOU HAPPY!", "ME WITH 'INSECURE ATTACHMENT' AS A LITTLE PUPPY DOG DESPERATE FOR ITS MASTER'S AFFECTION", and "MY 'SECURELY ATTACHED' BROTHER IN A NORMAL CHILDHOOD 'STROP'"]

I sometimes felt far too responsible as a teenage boy, as if I missed out on being a real teenager.

[Hand-drawn illustration: Two stick figures by a house — "LETS KNOCK ON THE DOOR AND RUN AWAY!" labelled "NORMAL BOYS' BEHAVIOUR". Next to it: "NOT FEELING ONE CAN BE A NORMAL TEENAGER AFFECTS PROPER DEVELOPMENT" — "I CAN'T, I MUST BE A GOOD BOY AND BE MY MOTHER'S 'MAN'. SHE WILL BE VERY SAD OTHERWISE", "I WAS ALWAYS PRE-OCCUPIED WITH THE NEED TO EMOTIONALLY SUPPORT MY MOTHER AT A YOUNG AGE"]

As a result, I used to subconsciously act like this later in life, which had a disastrous effect on my relationships with women.

PLEASE, NOTICE ME AND TELL ME I'M A GOOD PERSON, ATTRACTIVE, LOVEABLE, FUNNY AND WORTHY!

I SUBCONSCIOUSLY USED TO ACT LIKE THIS

KILLING YOUR OWN SOUL – THE EFFECTS OF TOXIC SHAME CONTAMINATION

A critical and fundamental source of poor, inbuilt low self-esteem is a significant overdose in childhood of toxic shame – this is a term coined by John Bradshaw in his excellent book *Healing the Shame That Binds You*. Shame is different from guilt in that guilt is, 'I did something bad', whereas shame is, 'I am bad, completely and fundamentally, to the core'. According to Bradshaw, shame is "the greatest form of learned domestic violence there is". Toxic shame can be deadly serious. In my first book I outlined its importance, but here I would like to discuss its implications and the effects it can have on a young child for the rest of its life, unless consciously acknowledged and adequately addressed. (I would be greatly interested to hear the thoughts of any reader on this topic as to me it's central to many of our problems).

As John Bradshaw points out, too much shame experienced by a child can become toxic when the child internalises the feeling of shame to such a degree that he feels overwhelmingly, that his/her own perceived deficiency and inadequacy is its cause. The child becomes as bound up in shame as a person tied round with rope. This leads you to despise your true essence or authentic self. It drives you to denigrate and destroy this authentic self to create a false self that you think will be more acceptable to the outside world. This can lead people to spend their whole lives in a tragic mindset. (For more on this topic search online for D. W. Winnicott who introduced the concept in the 1960s.) To my mind I went through the following stages to reach a state of toxic shame – please note that these stages are based purely on my own experiences and have no professional or academic grounding.

Starting point.

Happy kid, keen to please and love

Stages 1 to 4 (which happened very regularly, the effects of which build up drastically over time).

You're such a burden!

Shock, shame, self-doubt

You're driving me nuts

Fear of losing parent, shame

It's obviously all MY fault. I feel so sorry for my mother and father for having me

SELF-BLAME → SELF-LOATHING

I must destroy myself and build a more acceptable me

'SOUL MURDER' + CREATION OF FALSE SELF

Stage 5.

BANISHMENT OF REAL AUTHENTIC SELF, REPLACED BY FALSE SELF

Stage 6.

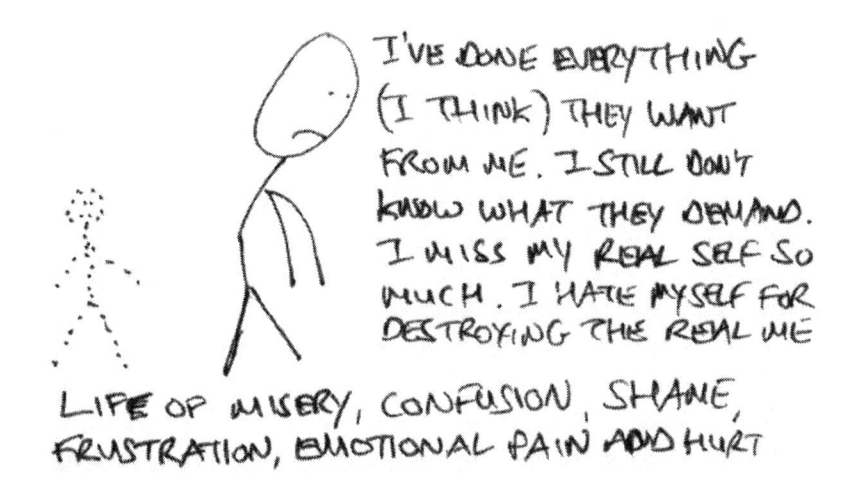

[Drawing of a sad stick figure with a dotted/disintegrating figure beside it, with handwritten text:]

I'VE DONE EVERYTHING (I THINK) THEY WANT FROM ME. I STILL DON'T KNOW WHAT THEY DEMAND. I MISS MY REAL SELF SO MUCH. I HATE MYSELF FOR DESTROYING THE REAL ME

LIFE OF MISERY, CONFUSION, SHAME, FRUSTRATION, EMOTIONAL PAIN AND HURT

I'd like to elaborate on some of these stages here. Being imbued with toxic shame as a child leads to what famed psychoanalyst Alice Miller described as "soul murder". This term to me means the desire to destroy the essence of a self that you regard with complete contempt. It's the desire to erase completely, and forever, everything about yourself.

Here I am committing soul murder.

[Three drawings of stick figures with handwritten labels:]

1. ME TRYING TO STAB AND KILL MY SOUL — MY SOUL, DAGGERS
2. ME THEN TRYING TO POISON MY SOUL — RAT POISON
3. THEN TRYING TO BURN WHATEVER IS LEFT OF MY REAL SELF

Toxic shame is dangerous.

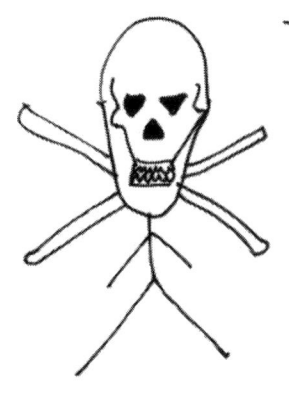

IT STRIPS YOU OF ANY COMPASSION FOR YOUR SELF, CONVINCES YOU THAT YOU ARE WORTH MUCH LESS THAN ANYONE ON THE PLANET WHO HAS EVER LIVED AND THEN CONVINCES YOU THAT YOU DON'T HAVE THE RIGHT TO EVER TALK ABOUT IT OR EVEN MENTION IT

It thrives like a virus if unrecognised and untreated.

MY FEARS TOOK ON A LIFE OF THEIR OWN LIKE AN UNTREATED VIRUS REPLICATING IN PERFECT DARK CONDITIONS CREATED BY TOXIC SHAME

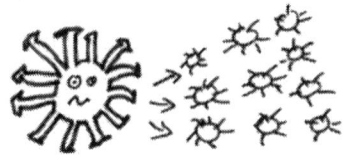

It thrives in silence.

THE LESS YOU TALK ABOUT IT, THE WORSE IT BECOMES, AND THE MORE EMBEDDED AND INTEGRATED IT BECOMES WITHIN YOU. IT BECOMES A FORM OF CANCER OF SELF-ESTEEM

Toxic shame drives the abandonment and isolation of your true self. As a child, this toxic shame had the effect of dragging me emotionally out to sea.

Dragged out to the sea to shame as a child

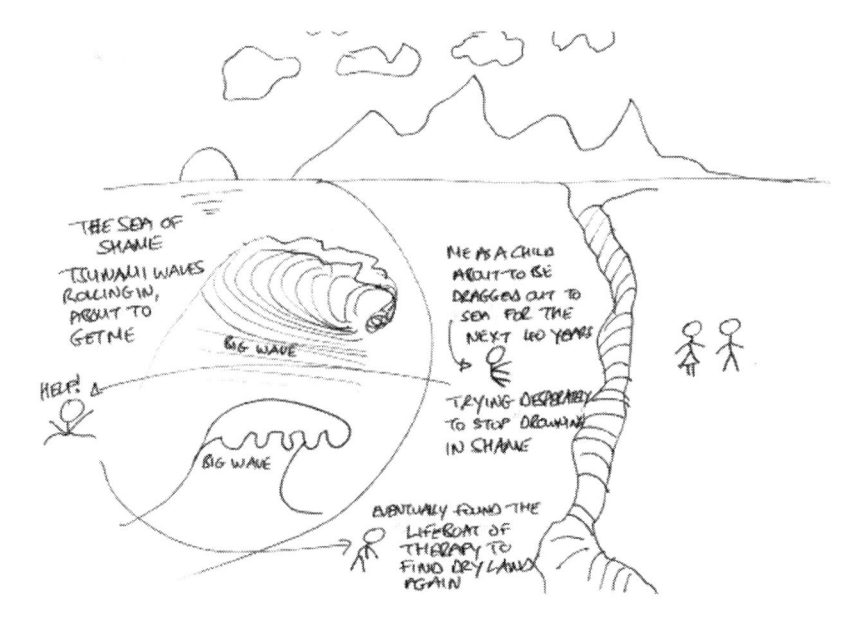

My parents are on the right of the picture, too distracted by their own issues to save me. They are standing on dry land, where people not submerged by toxic shame live.

Abandoning your authentic self on a desert island and creating a false self.

You have mixed emotions regarding your true, authentic and now abandoned self; on the one hand, you despise it as it seems so deficient and on the other hand you feel despair about having committed such an extreme and tragic act.

You feel internally very isolated and lonely and deep down very sad and confused but your 'Toxic Shame' drives your false self forward in life. No-one should ever find and the real and disgusting abandoned authentic me!!

This is of course all very disturbing for a child.

This is of course, deep down in the subconscious, heart-breaking for the child, especially when this extreme form of self-sacrifice seems to be ignored by everyone.

It's also very tiring playing a role that you feel has been assigned to you, but to no one else. Others can be themselves and ad lib in the play of life. (This is where 'transactional analysis' comes in, as discussed in my earlier book, where one follows a script for life, much like an actor playing a role.)

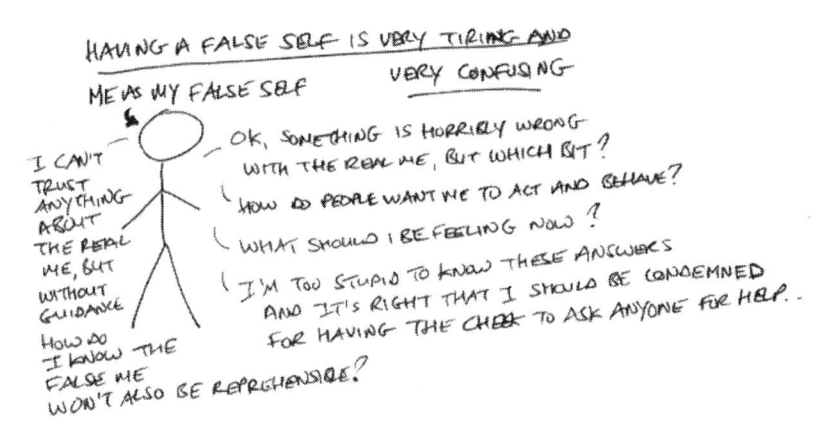

HAVING A FALSE SELF IS VERY TIRING AND VERY CONFUSING

ME AS MY FALSE SELF

- I CAN'T TRUST ANYTHING ABOUT THE REAL ME, BUT WITHOUT GUIDANCE HOW DO I KNOW THE FALSE ME WON'T ALSO BE REPREHENSIBLE?
- OK, SOMETHING IS HORRIBLY WRONG WITH THE REAL ME, BUT WHICH BIT?
- HOW DO PEOPLE WANT ME TO ACT AND BEHAVE?
- WHAT SHOULD I BE FEELING NOW?
- I'M TOO STUPID TO KNOW THESE ANSWERS AND IT'S RIGHT THAT I SHOULD BE CONDEMNED FOR HAVING THE CHEEK TO ASK ANYONE FOR HELP.

It feels emotionally and behaviourally very restrictive. I felt like I was mentally in a straitjacket, within a series of Russian dolls outer layers severely restricting myself in what I could/was allowed to think about.

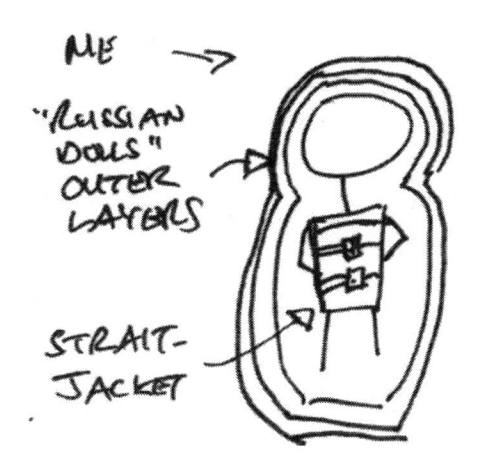

ME → "RUSSIAN DOLLS" OUTER LAYERS — STRAIT-JACKET

Because you feel permanent shame about who and what you are, you are always looking to prove your worth and to make amends.

50   How to Sort Your Head Out

[Illustration: Three stick figures. Thought bubble from left figure: "WOW, THESE PEOPLE APPEAR FLAWLESS AND I'M WORSE THAN HITLER OR STALIN." Label above middle figures: "RANDOM PEOPLE". Text at top right: "TOXIC SHAME MEANS YOU ARE ALWAYS TRYING TO PROVE THAT YOU ARE MAKING AMENDS FOR YOUR ORIGINAL SIN. YOU BELIEVE EVERYONE ELSE IS AMAZING AND YOU ARE THE OPPOSITE". Lower caption: "I MUST PROVE TO THEM THAT I'M WORTHY OF THEIR ATTENTION WHILE ALSO SHOWING COMPLETE MEEKNESS AND SUBJUGATION AS A FORM OF APOLOGY FOR BEING ME"]

[Illustration: Three stick figures with text: "I WOULD CARRY ON THIS BEHAVIOUR FOR THE REST OF MY LIFE, ALWAYS TRYING TO INGRATIATE PEOPLE AND LAUGH AT THEIR JOKES"]

I also had real pangs of shame for little obvious reason.

[Illustration: A house with two stick figures beside it, labelled "MY BROTHER AT HIS FRIEND'S HOUSE, WHO WE OFTEN VISITED". A stick figure below with text: "I'M SO ASHAMED, HAVING TO HANG OUT WITH A FRIEND OF MY YOUNGER BROTHER'S"]

Feeling 'pre-shamed' had bizarre consequences for me, such as admitting to bullying a boy in school when I had absolutely nothing to do with it (quite the opposite in fact).

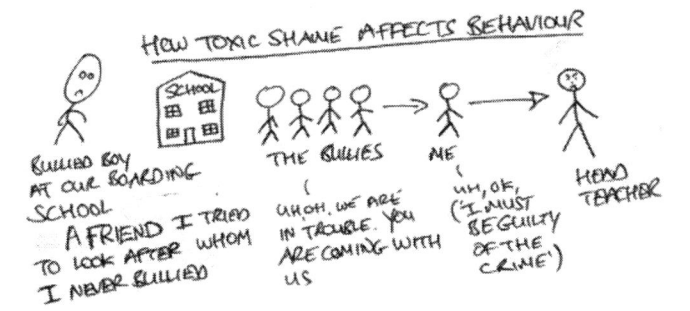

UNDERSTANDING THINGS FURTHER TO FULLY SAVE YOURSELF   51

I compare the experience of childhood toxic shame with playing a game of Snakes and Ladders in which the shamed child believes that he/she is only worthy of landing on the squares with snakes and therefore actively seeks them out as a form of masochistic punishment.

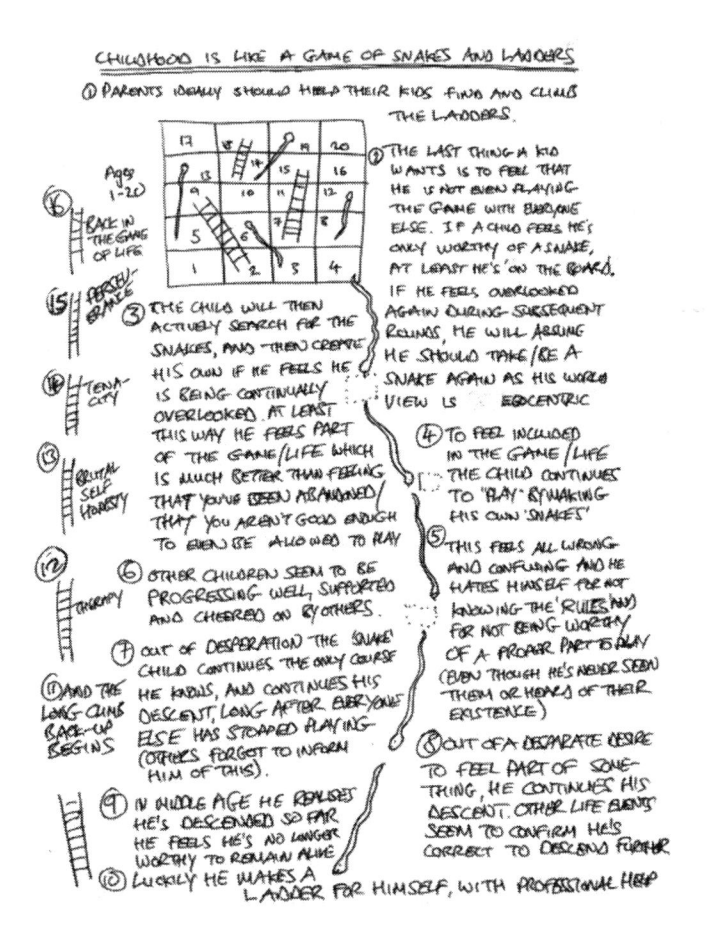

The tree below represents how toxic shame, depicted here as infected roots of a tree, manifests itself negatively throughout the life cycle of the whole organism (the tree representing a person in this instance).

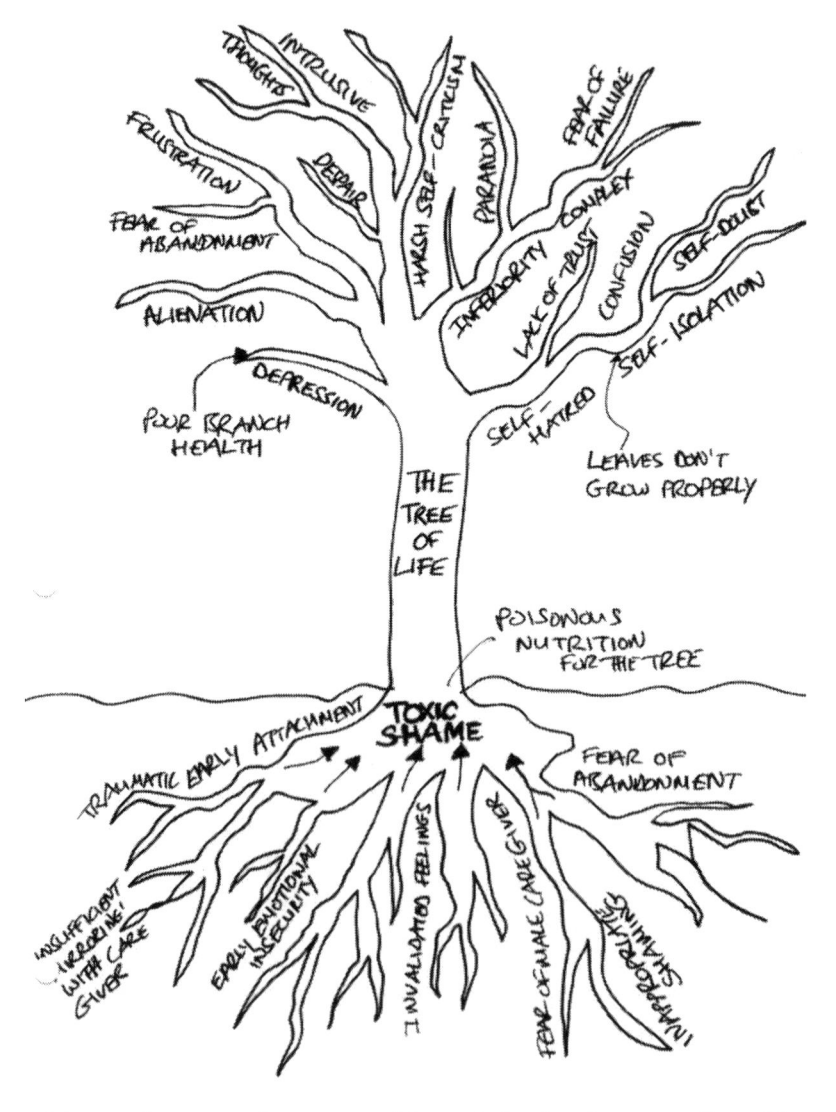

I felt very insecure about my self-worth in the absence of positive emotional interaction with my parents and others. I therefore had to construct some form of identity to give me something to hold onto as simply not knowing anything about my perceived value as a human being was frightening and very confusing for me. I defined myself as being a shame-based person – 'I'm bad to the core, it's just who I am.' To some extent this had to happen to me as I had little emotional feedback from my own parents/grown wounded children. Absence of any feedback is dreadful – a child is desperate to know who/what it is, so at least I had something to define myself/hold on to.

So, I defined myself through shame and I became *Shameman*.

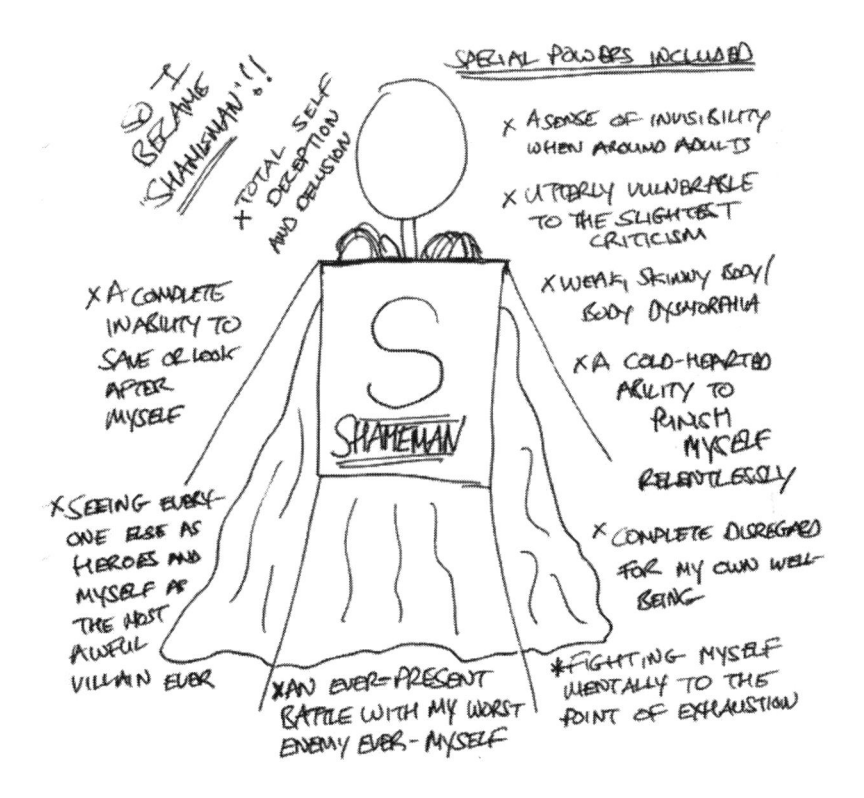

SHAMEMAN!!
+ TOTAL SELF DECEPTION AND DELUSION

SPECIAL POWERS INCLUDED

× A SENSE OF INVISIBILITY WHEN AROUND ADULTS

× UTTERLY VULNERABLE TO THE SLIGHTEST CRITICISM

× A COMPLETE INABILITY TO SAVE OR LOOK AFTER MYSELF

× WEAK, SKINNY BODY / BODY DYSMORPHIA

× A COLD-HEARTED ABILITY TO PUNISH MYSELF RELENTLESSLY

× SEEING EVERYONE ELSE AS HEROES AND MYSELF AS THE MOST AWFUL VILLAIN EVER

× COMPLETE DISREGARD FOR MY OWN WELL BEING

× AN EVER-PRESENT BATTLE WITH MY WORST ENEMY EVER - MYSELF

* FIGHTING MYSELF MENTALLY TO THE POINT OF EXHAUSTION

Having all these negative emotions churning away inside you is very energy-sapping and confusing.

Toxic shame led to a churning, washing machine of emotions in my mind, with thoughts and emotions spinning around inside me. I would feel too scared and ashamed to open the door and for the real world to see my fears and awful, dirty me.

[Drawing of a stick figure with a box-shaped head containing swirling thoughts]

These churning thoughts and emotions of mine included the following:

THESE CHURNING THOUGHTS AND EMOTIONS INCLUDE:

- 'I WENT TO GREAT LENGTHS TO DESTROY MY AUTHENTIC SELF AND CREATE A NEW SELF TO PLEASE MY PARENTS AND OTHERS, BUT NO-ONE SEEMS TO NOTICE — FRUSTRATING!'
- 'NOBODY EVER TOLD ME WHAT WAS SO WRONG WITH ME, BUT I CAN'T RETURN TO MY REAL SELF AS THAT WILL DRIVE PEOPLE AWAY. I'M CAUGHT IN LIMBO — NO RETURN TO REAL SELF AND ACTING OUT MY (FALSE) NEW SELF IS SIMPLY TOO EXHAUSTING WITH NO BENEFITS.'
- 'I FEEL PRIDE FOR DOING WHAT (I THINK) MY PARENTS WANTED, BUT ALSO HUMILIATION AND REGRET FOR HAVING 'MURDERED' MY SOUL'

Negative, shame-filled thoughts can run wild in a child's mind.

A SCARED CHILD'S MIND IS LIKE A STARTLED HORSE

IT WILL JUST RUN AND RUN FOR MILES, WITH NO DIRECTION AND NO IDEA WHERE IT WILL END UP

As a result, a child's ability to shame itself knows almost no bounds and he/she can create an emotional 'well' for itself where it believes it belongs. When you are infected with toxic shame as a child, before you have been able to build any picture of your own self-worth, or your place in the world, then the 'fall' can be almost infinite as there is nothing to stop your demise.

The picture below depicts me in my well of despair as a child from where it was my task to put everyone else first and to never look after myself. Due to a combination of factors I chose to jump into the well as I thought this was where I belonged. I believed that the whole world shared this view. It was of course a very lonely place to be. My toxic shame made me believe that I was ripe for mockery, so I imagined everyone else looking down at me and abusing me. The longer you hold the feelings about yourself, the harder it is to escape, especially as they become hardened and fossilised in your mind.

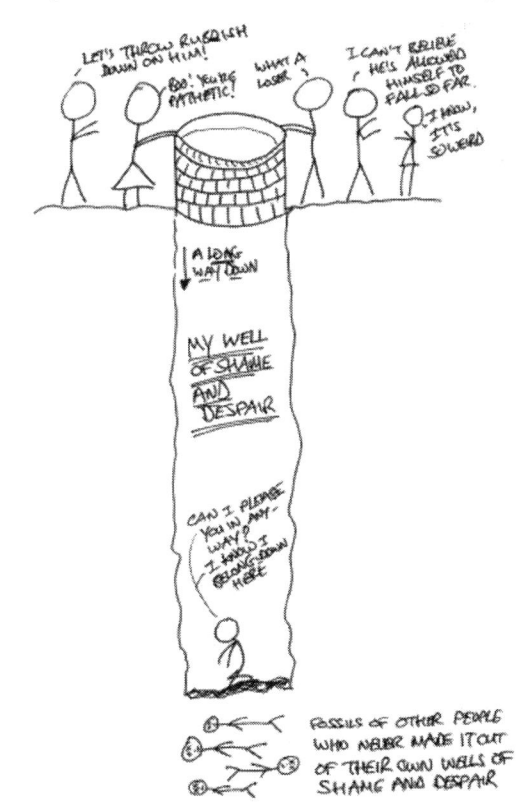

SHAMED, FEARFUL CHILDREN ARE RIPE FOR RELIGIOUS INDOCTRINATION

Christianity's teaching of original sin has much in common with toxic shame in that God and the person who happens to be shaming the child in question are conveying similar messages. In essence, both offer love on a conditional basis only, in the following ways:

- I have complete power and moral authority over you and I cannot be questioned
- I am the ultimate arbiter and judge of your legitimacy as a human being and your right to be alive
- You must please me to gain legitimacy, acceptance and to be saved from death.
- However, you will always be tainted by your inherent sin/shamefulness, no matter how hard you try to overcome it, but try you must as failure is too scary to contemplate
- I will never clarify how you can make amends for your inherent state of sin/shame, but you must make amends nevertheless.

Original sin, a key tenet of Christian teaching, is a form of toxic shame to my mind.

ADAM AND EVE ATE FROM THE TREE OF KNOWLEDGE BECAUSE OF A TALKING SNAKE

I was told as a child that because of Adam and Eve's actions, I was born a sinner, infected with an ancient spiritual disease and defective as a result, and that I would inevitably disappoint God by disobeying him because of inherited sin, passed down the millennia. (See Roman Catholic doctrine at http://www.vatican.va/archive/ENG0015/__P1C.HTM) I was then told that I could only be saved through the grace of God for these transgressions. In the words of the late Christopher Hitchens, "Born sick, but commanded to be well". Because of my family life I was susceptible to such a message. This accusation against me from people I trusted, namely the nuns teaching me in my first school, had a profound and damaging effect on my inherent sense of value as a person, until I finally found the courage to challenge this claim in my middle age.

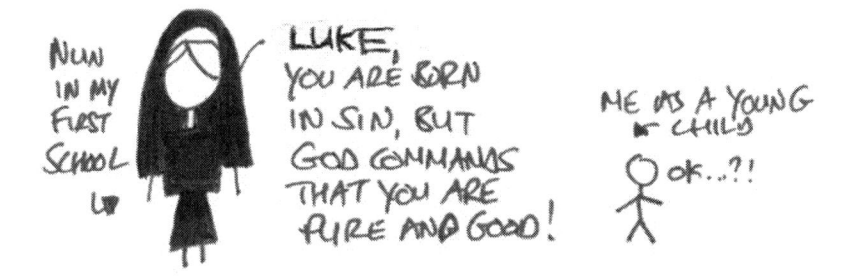

[Illustration: A nun labelled "NUN IN MY FIRST SCHOOL" saying "LUKE, YOU ARE BORN IN SIN, BUT GOD COMMANDS THAT YOU ARE PURE AND GOOD!" to a stick figure labelled "ME AS A YOUNG CHILD" replying "ok..?!"]

Because of the combination of these experiences at home and school I felt unfairly victimised by all those I looked up to (parents, teachers and God himself), especially as I was trying so hard to please everyone. The fact that God himself seemed disappointed in me before my life had even properly begun was difficult for me as a child to conceptualise.

I imagined God telling me the following: You, Luke Pemberton, I'm watching and scrutinising you only! You cannot be trusted. You need constant oversight because you are a poor, lowly sinner who has failed his parents in the most fundamental way possible! No matter how hard you try to make amends for your trespasses, it will never be enough and I will always be on hand to punish you at the slightest misdemeanour. I will let everyone else be weak, sinful and treacherous. But not you, who will never have a moment's rest from my permanent and judgemental gaze. There will be no respite from me and no explanation ever.

I felt victimised, and wholly unjustifiably signed out for unjust scrutiny when I was trying so hard every day to be an ideal son and 'Child of God', and very fearful.

<figure>
ALL POWERFUL — PERFECT — ALL KNOWING
GOD
↓
Me / other people all over the world, good, bad, normal — 7,000,000,000
</figure>

These religious-oriented experiences will no doubt only feel familiar to a limited number of us (although I may be underestimating this assessment somewhat).

THOUGHTS THAT SCARE YOU – OBSESSIVE COMPULSIVE DISORDER

One of the more upsetting side-effects of negative childhood experiences are regular, distressing thoughts that intrude on daily functioning. (See https://www.intrusivethoughts.org/ocd-symptoms/harm-ocd/ and also https://en.wikipedia.org/wiki/Intrusive_thought and https://iocdf.org/ and https://iocdf.org/about-ocd/) In the course of psychotherapy while trying to address and work through my issues, I regularly experienced troubling thoughts and urges. This notion of intrusive thoughts is perhaps something that all of us can associate with to some degree, although to my mind it's one of the trickiest things to talk about as I felt I was the only one thinking weird thoughts. These included:

STEPPING IN FRONT OF AN ONCOMING TRAIN

BEING DEAD IN A GRAVE

CUTTING MYSELF WITH KNIVES, INCLUDING CHOPPING MY HAND OFF IN ONE GO

[Drawing: stick figure hitting another, labeled "Ow!" with caption "COMMITTING RANDOM ACTS OF VIOLENCE AGAINST INNOCENT PEOPLE"]

Luckily a person close to me recommended the excellent website www.intrusivethoughts.org which groups such thinking into a number of categories including the following:

Scrupulosity OCD – the fear of being punished for blasphemy.

Because I believed when I was growing up that God could hear and see my every thought, I found myself almost constantly asking for God's forgiveness and mentally repeating prayers.

[Drawing titled "SCRUPULOSITY OCD" with a cross, and stick figure thinking "THOU SHALT NOT SIN, THOU SHALT NOT SIN, THOU SHALT NOT SIN"]

As a child I would often pray/beg for God's forgiveness, often for tiny infractions and for merely thinking something.

This sense of permanent intrusion on private thoughts, and the threat of eternal judgement, is awful to experience.

Space in my mind to think freely became increasingly restricted and controlled by me so as not to "sin".

In the end I only allowed myself a tiny space to think good thoughts.

Sub conscious

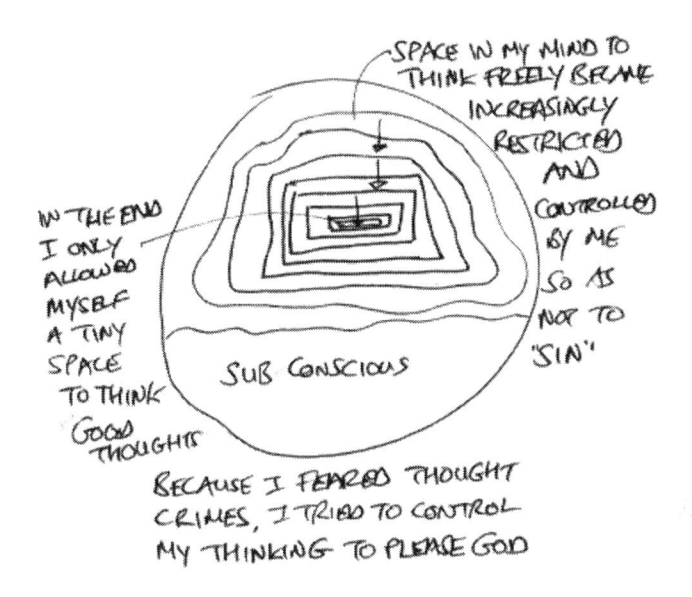

Because I feared thought crimes, I tried to control my thinking to please God.

Homosexuality OCD.

Because I was so desperate to connect with male figures when I was growing up, my subconscious thinking was that I would do pretty much anything to obtain this connection and sense of acceptance. When your brain functions like this, I gather it often considers sexually submissive acts as the final desperate bid to gain what you crave.

As a result, when walking down the street I would have fleeting images of me giving oral sex to a man who happened to walk past (a total stranger). These were very disturbing for me, who had never found men attractive.

Partly because of these subconscious urges coming to the fore, later in life I would have homosexual intrusive thoughts, even though I had never found men sexually attractive.

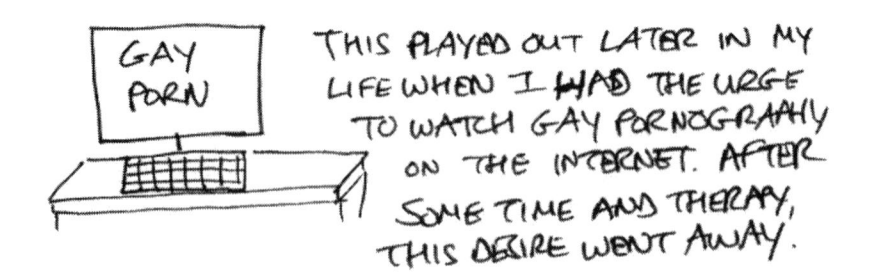

As mentioned elsewhere, I also, for a certain period, had homosexual urges which confused me a lot.

This played out later in my life when I had the urge to watch gay pornography on the internet. After some time and therapy, this desire went away.

Relationship OCD.

I developed something called relationship obsessive-compulsive disorder later in life. This has been described in the following way: "When you have OCD, recurring unwanted thoughts that you're not worthy of love, you're not good enough for your partner or that you might not even love your partner are amplified. You may even go so far as to believe that your partner or spouse is cheating on you."

RELATIONSHIP OCD

MY WIFE — OTHER MAN

DESPITE BEING MARRIED TO A WONDERFUL, HONEST, KIND AND DEDICATED WIFE I WOULD OFTEN HAVE FLEETING THOUGHTS OF HER LEAVING ME, TOTALLY UNJUSTIFIED AND DELUSIONAL

Shamed, anxious people with a poor self-image are more susceptible to such intrusive thoughts. Many people perhaps have some of these thoughts passing through their mind occasionally, but with anxious, OCD people the alarm bells start ringing inside their heads and they react with increased anxiety and concern to a fleeting thought or a 'creative association'. This leads to a vicious cycle of focusing on these thoughts, which perpetuates the anxiety that they may actually represent something serious. In fact, such thoughts are often completely meaningless 'creative associations' that all brains occasionally produce. If one is particularly shamed, with low self-esteem and in a depression with burnout, this vicious cycle can start quickly and be very upsetting.

According to Dr. Steven Phillipson (www.intrusivethoughts.org/living-intrusive-thoughts/) such disturbing thoughts are "generally almost the exact opposite in terms of a person's character. The targets of the spike theme are just a fabrication of the malfunctioning brain. And there is no authentic belief system within the person related to those associations."

Dr Hannah Reese says that "sometimes thoughts like these come to us precisely because we do not want to act in this way; they are simply the most inappropriate thing your mind can imagine." (www.psychologytoday.com/blog/am-i-normal/201110/intrusive-thoughts-normal-or-not) The emotional stress and general anxiety I was experiencing, because of my past trauma, meant that my panicked efforts to get these thoughts out of my mind just made the whole situation worse, as thinking about them kept them ever present. Dr Hannah Reese again: "When someone becomes very distressed by their intrusive thoughts, goes to great lengths to get rid of them, and prevent them from occurring, this can become a form of Obsessive Compulsive Disorder (OCD)."

LOST AND SCARED IN AN IMPOSSIBLE EMOTIONAL MAZE

The combination of experiences described in the preceding pages results in a child feeling lost as if in a maze.

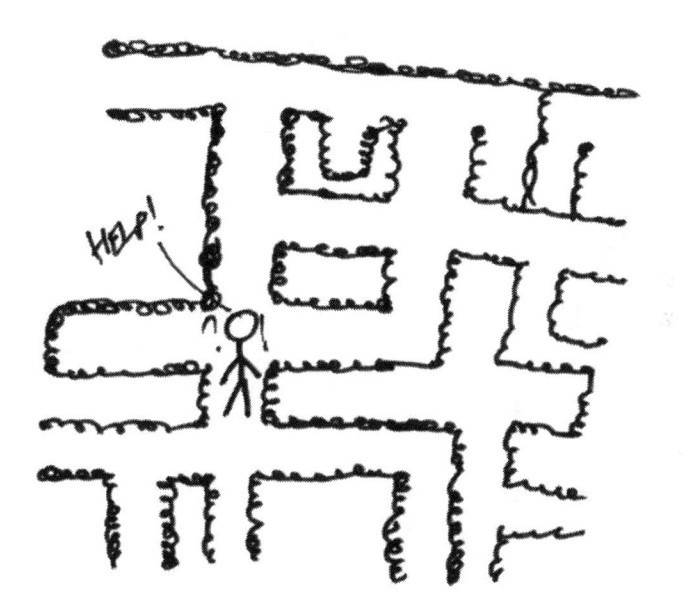

The huge, complex maze has really high hedges and is created in the child's mind by confusing and contradictory behaviour by the primary care givers. It's like putting a small, scared child into such a structure, and then telling them all his/her family members and friends are having a party outside of its boundaries, implying that they're too stupid to find the exit and join the party.

This sense of isolation and being fenced-off led to my feeling lost and emotionally disconnected and adrift from family and friends.

66 How to Sort Your Head Out

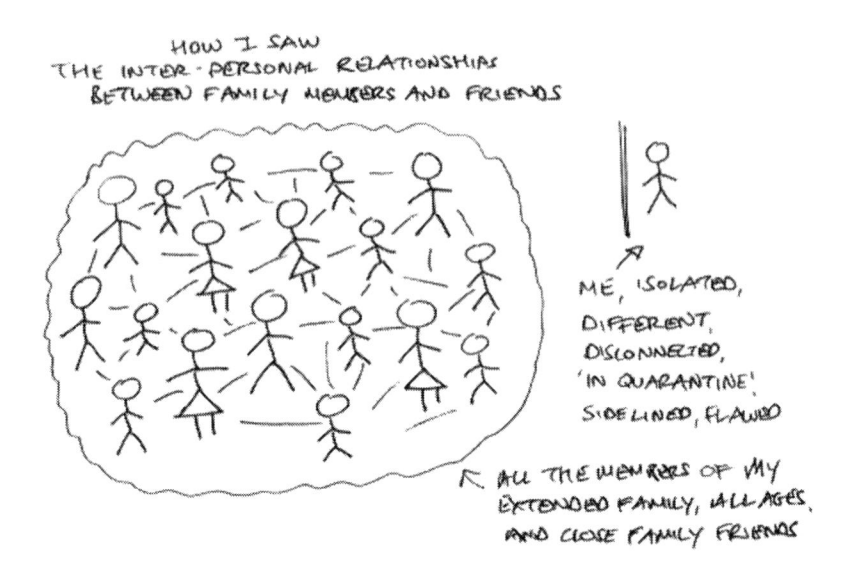

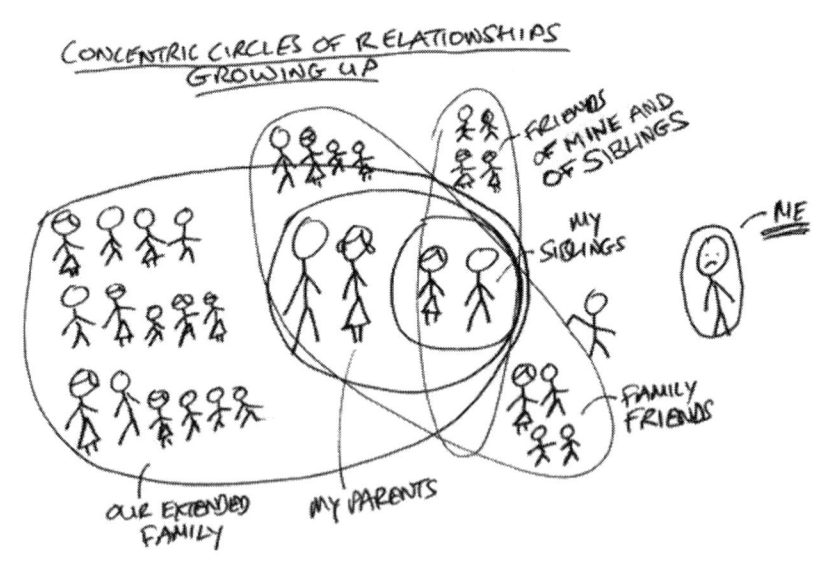

How I saw the inter-personal relationships between family members and friends

Me, isolated, different, disconnected, 'in quarantine', sidelined, flawed

All the members of my extended family, all ages, and close family friends

Concentric circles of relationships growing up

Friends of mine and of siblings

My siblings

Me

Family friends

Our extended family

My parents

I always felt like I wasn't good enough to be allowed to be a member of any group and, as a result, I tended to feel isolated and different from everybody. As well as me in the bubble on the right, I am also represented trying to knock on the outside of one of the barriers, asking to be granted entry on occasion (if good enough and allowed).

Self-isolation can sometimes be very hard to bear.

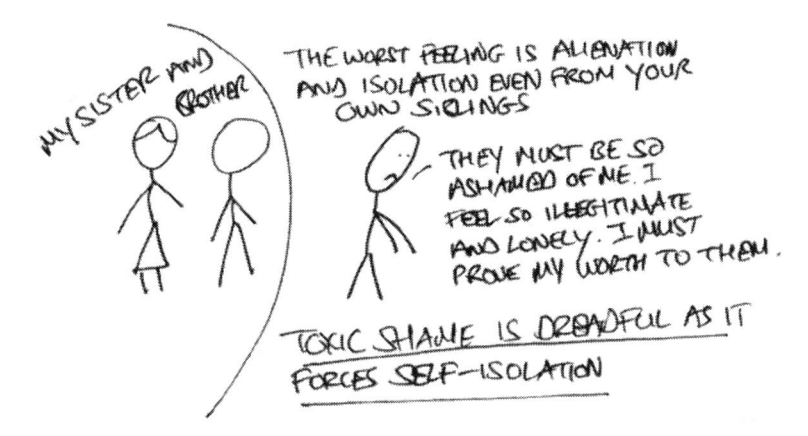

MY SISTER AND BROTHER

THE WORST FEELING IS ALIENATION AND ISOLATION EVEN FROM YOUR OWN SIBLINGS

THEY MUST BE SO ASHAMED OF ME. I FEEL SO ILLEGITIMATE AND LONELY. I MUST PROVE MY WORTH TO THEM.

TOXIC SHAME IS DREADFUL AS IT FORCES SELF-ISOLATION

I still feel anxious when I speak to my brother on the phone, which is ridiculous, as he's a lovely, generous person. I realise I'm subconsciously still scared of disappointing and losing him. It just goes to show the long-term effect negative childhood experiences can have on you.

MY BROTHER

ME

I MUST PROVE MY WORTH TO HIM AGAIN

EVEN NOW I STILL FEEL ANXIOUS WHEN I TALK TO MY YOUNGER BROTHER ON THE TELEPHONE (RIDICULOUS, AS HE IS A VERY KIND AND GENEROUS PERSON)

I did however feel connected to a small group of close friends from my childhood, which was an immense help. However, I was very fearful of anyone outside this small circle of close friends whom I trusted very much (and still do).

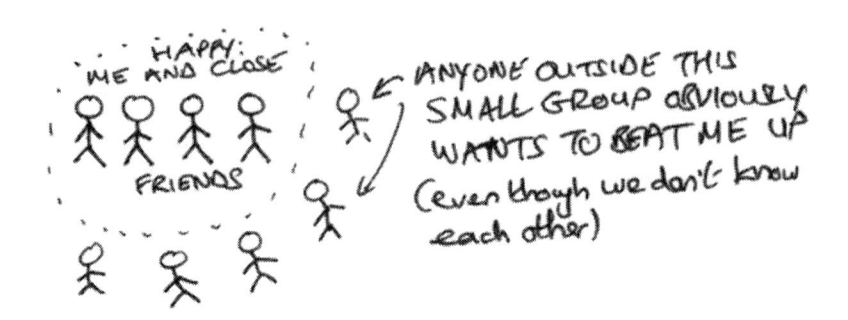

At the end of childhood, I had the sense of being the only unwanted product on a supermarket shelf, past its sell-by date, made of unpleasant ingredients.

Me as a milk carton...

... sitting on a supermarket shelf.

At the end of childhood, I felt like the only product left on a super market which was closing for good. I assumed I must be made of disgusting ingredients contained within awful, damaged packaging, past my sell-by date, and poisonous to others thinking people were right not to choose me from the shelf.

THE SUPERMARKET OF LIFE

Rows of empty shelves — All the other boys + girls on the shelves had been chosen long ago by their parents and other friends — It seemed like no-one wanted me — that I had been forgotten about — ME — SALE! 90% DISCOUNT EVERYTHING MUST GO!

These experiences made me feel emotionally very insecure.

I remember being about eleven or twelve staying at a friend's house when I suddenly had a desperate desire to go home and sleep in my own bed.

I would as a child suddenly feel desperately insecure e.g. when at a friend's house for a sleepover, for no reason whatsoever.

14:00 — ? — I would really like to go home now, please! — Luke, don't you want to keep playing games? — Room with great games + lovely big garden — Good friend of mine — My friend's lovely mother — ME

The problem is that one's first, broad understanding of value as a person becomes embedded and fixed in one's mind.

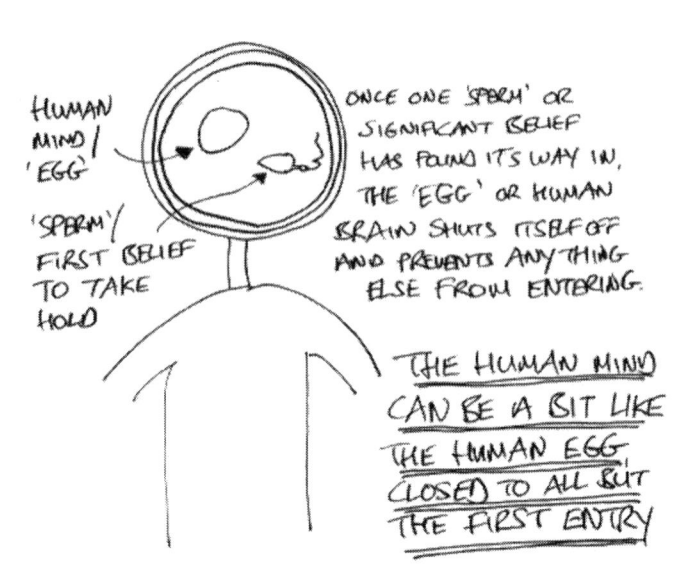

[Diagram: "HUMAN MIND / 'EGG'" with "'SPERM' / FIRST BELIEF TO TAKE HOLD" entering. Caption: "ONCE ONE 'SPERM' OR SIGNIFICANT BELIEF HAS FOUND ITS WAY IN, THE 'EGG' OR HUMAN BRAIN SHUTS ITSELF OFF AND PREVENTS ANYTHING ELSE FROM ENTERING."]

THE HUMAN MIND CAN BE A BIT LIKE THE HUMAN EGG CLOSED TO ALL BUT THE FIRST ENTRY

I felt unprepared emotionally for life, and very vulnerable (another common feeling to many of us, of course).

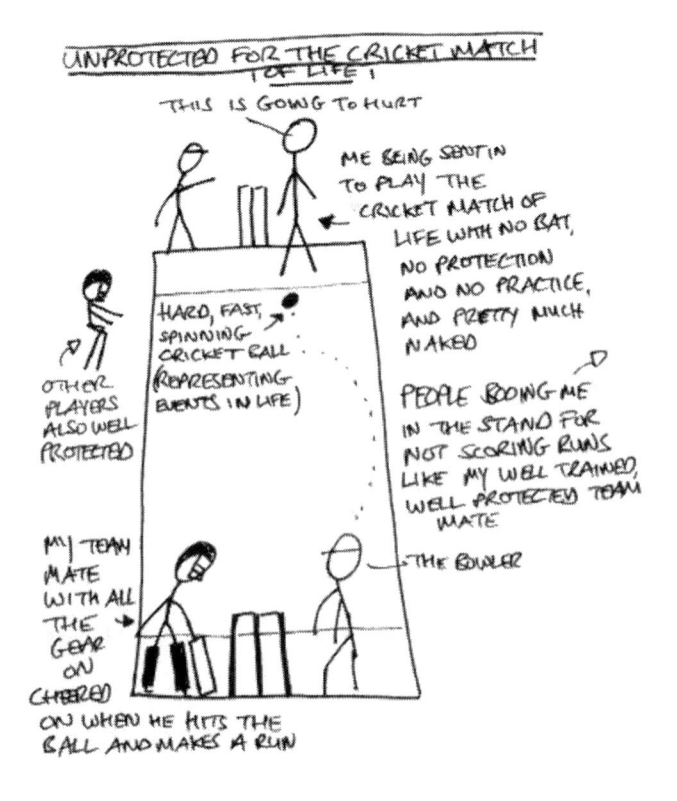

[Diagram: "UNPROTECTED FOR THE CRICKET MATCH OF LIFE!"
- *"THIS IS GOING TO HURT"*
- *"ME BEING SENT IN TO PLAY THE CRICKET MATCH OF LIFE WITH NO BAT, NO PROTECTION AND NO PRACTICE, AND PRETTY MUCH NAKED"*
- *"HARD, FAST, SPINNING CRICKET BALL (REPRESENTING EVENTS IN LIFE)"*
- *"OTHER PLAYERS ALSO WELL PROTECTED"*
- *"PEOPLE BOOING ME IN THE STAND FOR NOT SCORING RUNS LIKE MY WELL TRAINED, WELL PROTECTED TEAM MATE"*
- *"THE BOWLER"*
- *"MY TEAM MATE WITH ALL THE GEAR ON CHEERED ON WHEN HE HITS THE BALL AND MAKES A RUN"]*

UNDERSTANDING THINGS FURTHER TO FULLY SAVE YOURSELF   71

ME HIDING IN A FOREST ON A SCHOOL TRIP TO FRANCE

OTHER PUPILS CHATTING AND MESSING AROUND

FEELING SO VULNERABLE, TOTALLY INSECURE, ISOLATED, HELPLESS

I WOULD SOMETIMES FEEL ACUTELY JEALOUS OF A BABY IN A PRAM WHO HAD THE TOTAL BELOVED ATTENTION OF ITS MOTHER

FRIENDS CHATTING

I WOULD OFTEN FIND MYSELF STUDYING HOW PEOPLE BEHAVED IN SOCIAL SITUATIONS TO LEARN HOW I COULD ATTRACT AND KEEP THE ATTENTION OF OTHER PEOPLE

These negative experiences can lead to catastrophising – the expectation that anything good may disappear at any moment.

Later on in life I would find myself 'catastrophising':

I'm so glad that happened to me

Shortly afterwards →

That must mean that something catastrophic is going to happen now – nuclear war perhaps?

I had set off in totally the wrong direction emotionally in life and unfortunately didn't get the regular direction corrections needed to find my way to a place of proper self-esteem.

WARNING! YOU ARE UNDER CONSTANT CCTV SURVEILLANCE

I always felt that I was being scrutinised and judged, and if I did not try to put other people first 100% then I would be condemned humiliatingly

Uh, oh... I really need to be 'on form' and make a good impression

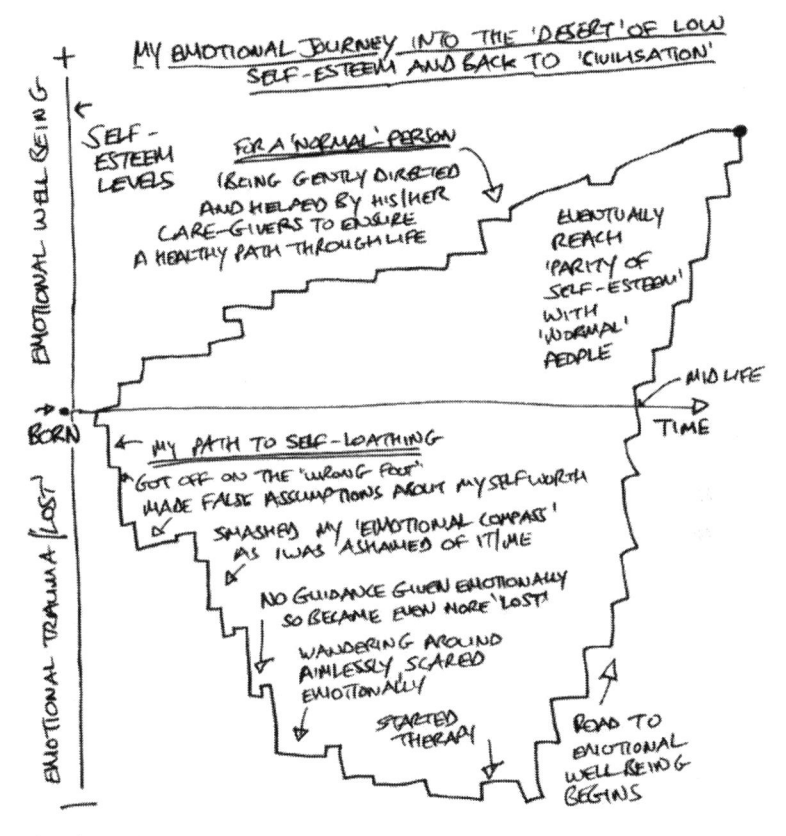

Indeed, I still have a deep, irrational and wholly unjustified fear of abandonment – as everyone does, of course, to some degree, but some of us have it to a painful and frightening extent.

It never occurred to me that I should put myself first in any scenario.

What I was (sub-consciously) thinking at parties

"If I can make sure everyone here feels very comfortable, at least, and happy, then I can relax a bit myself"

Because of my unrestrained, underdeveloped, fearful and confused child's mind I created subconsciously many rules that I thought applied to me only.

My Own 10 Commandments

1. Other people are **much better than you** are and are worth more than you – always remember this; you were rejected as a child for good reason – you are just not up to scratch.

2. Everybody is **aware of and shares your innermost view** of the world – that you are a disgusting human being and that you must work very hard, all the time, to make amends for being so deficient and disappointing to so many people.
3. People are **right to treat you with animosity**, contempt, criticism and to dismiss you out of hand – it serves you right for being who you are; if people decide to grant you their friendship or pay you the slightest bit of attention, be very grateful as you don't deserve it.
4. Never put yourself first – always subjugate your own needs to those of other people; only think about your own needs if and when everybody else is content and satisfied, and then only in the briefest manner; submissiveness, shame, meekness and obedience should be your watch words.
5. Never give yourself the time and space to love yourself, this is just not acceptable – any attempt to do so should be met with the utmost shame.
6. Fear your own feelings, especially anger, as it will turn people away from you.
7. You alone among everyone else will be continuously scrutinised in the most intrusive manner for your behaviour; should you detract in the slightest manner from the behaviour demanded of you, you will be punished immediately and without warning.
8. Never dare to question any of the above or ask for any explanation – you are a sinner and you will be severely punished for doing so, including not being allowed into heaven when you die.
9. There is no escape from this constant supervision as you cannot be allowed to have your own life, you are forever condemned to suffer.
10. Your only way to salvation/redemption is through continued self-sacrifice and submissiveness – any other course of action will not be tolerated.

HOW THESE EMOTIONAL EXPERIENCES MANIFESTED THEMSELVES IN ADULTHOOD

The big question in my mind for my entire life was ....

...Why did my parents, and God, seem to approve of everyone else except me? I felt unfairly victimised.

What having toxic shame feels like as an adult.

Remember feeling excruciating, painful shame as a child that made you feel unbelievably self-conscious and vulnerable? Well, as an adult you continue to have these feelings in the back of your mind pretty much every waking moment (without wishing to be overly dramatic about it). I wonder how many readers can relate to this?

I believed I was worth a lot less as a person than other people.

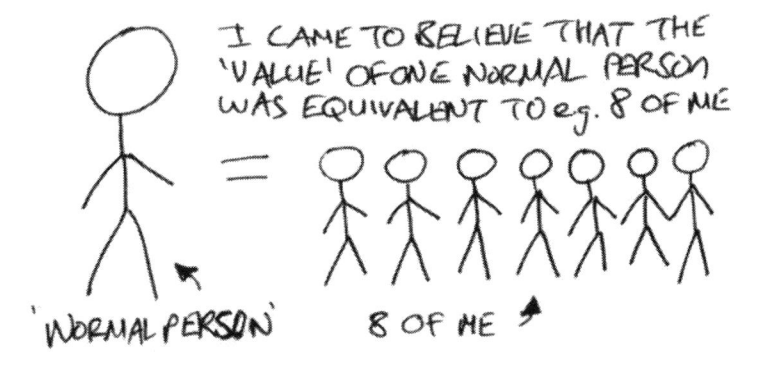

78   How to Sort Your Head Out

'NORMAL PERSON' = *I BELIEVED IF I TRIED 8 TIMES AS HARD AS A 'NORMAL PERSON' THEN I COULD BE AS VALUABLE AS THEM*

ME TRYING TO BE AS GOOD AS AN ANGEL AND SWEATING FROM TRYING SO HARD

FRIENDS AT PARTIES HAVING GREAT FUN, BEING THEMSELVES

ME FLEEING THE PARTY OUT OF ACUTE ANXIETY

<u>I OFTEN HAD THE 'FLIGHT' INSTINCT AT SOCIAL GATHERINGS</u>

After university, and my parents' divorce, I travelled through Southeast Asia and on to Australia with friends. At a great New Year's Eve party in Sydney in the mid-1990s I suddenly, out of the blue, burst into floods of tears just as the clock struck midnight and everyone started celebrating wildly. I think the sight of everyone looking so confident and happy reminded me of my own sense of despair, which became overwhelming at that moment.

NYE SYDNEY 00:00

ME BREAKING DOWN IN TEARS

HURRAY! HAPPY NEW YEAR! KISS ME! WHAT A GREAT FEELING! PARTY!

Although I got married to a wonderful woman and we had two beautiful children, I still felt very paranoid and worthless, to say the least.

I used to believe I was totally inconsequential and that my own family would have seamlessly moved on with their lives if I had suddenly disappeared one day (totally delusional of course).

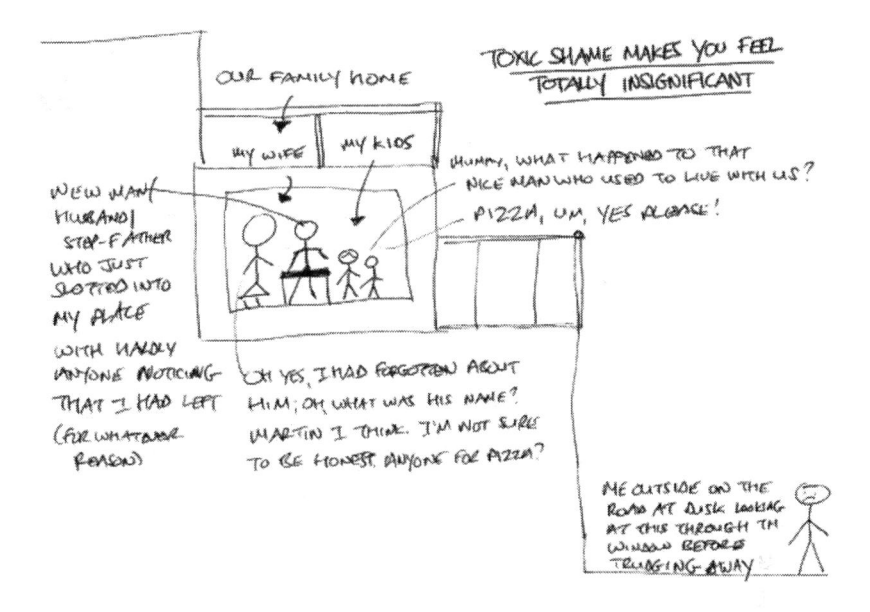

TOXIC SHAME MAKES YOU FEEL TOTALLY INSIGNIFICANT

OUR FAMILY HOME

MY WIFE | MY KIDS

NEW MAN/ HUSBAND/ STEP-FATHER WHO JUST SLOTTED INTO MY PLACE WITH HARDLY ANYONE NOTICING THAT I HAD LEFT (FOR WHATEVER REASON)

MUMMY, WHAT HAPPENED TO THAT NICE MAN WHO USED TO LIVE WITH US?

PIZZA, UM, YES PLEASE!

OH YES, I HAD FORGOTTEN ABOUT HIM; OH WHAT WAS HIS NAME? MARTIN I THINK. I'M NOT SURE TO BE HONEST. ANYONE FOR PIZZA?

ME OUTSIDE ON THE ROAD AT DUSK LOOKING AT THIS THROUGH THE WINDOW BEFORE TRUDGING AWAY

A PERMANENT STATE OF MENTAL EXHAUSTION

This despair and its causes is exhausting to deal with daily. I have tried to summarise this below.

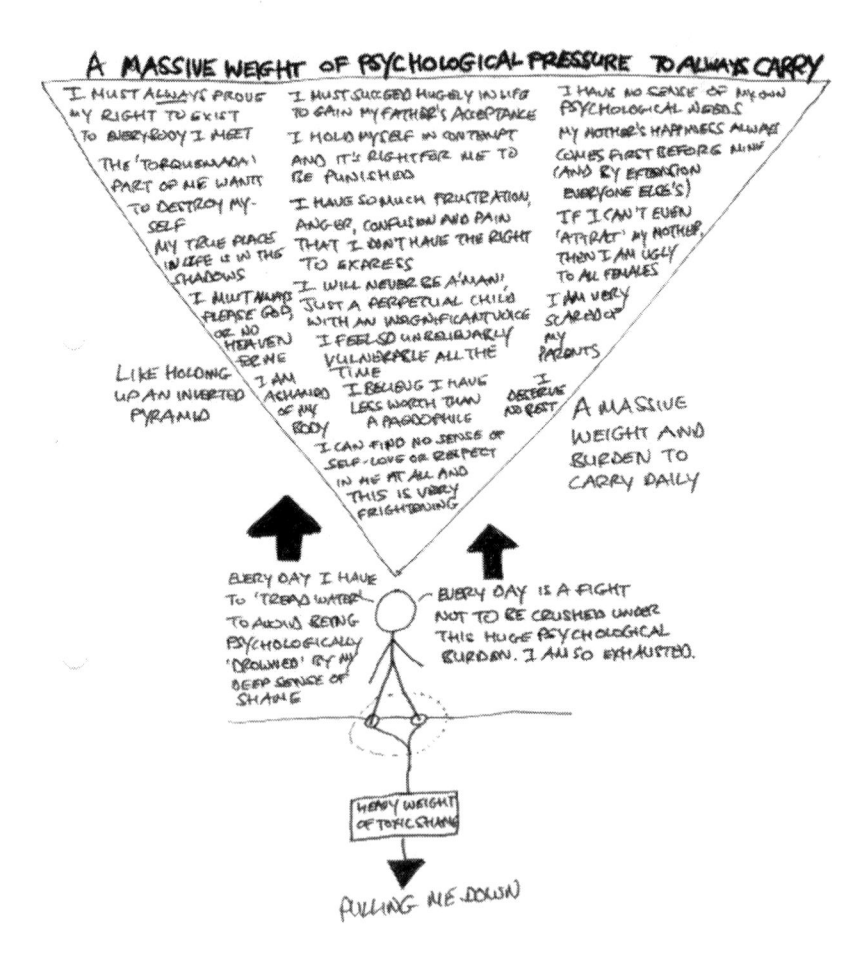

A MASSIVE WEIGHT OF PSYCHOLOGICAL PRESSURE TO ALWAYS CARRY

- I must always prove my right to exist to everybody I meet
- The 'Torquemada' part of me wants to destroy myself
- My true place in life is in the shadows
- I must always please God or no heaven for me
- Like holding up an inverted pyramid
- I am ashamed of my body
- I must succeed hugely in life to gain my father's acceptance
- I hold myself in contempt and it's right for me to be punished
- I have so much frustration, anger, confusion and pain that I don't have the right to express
- I will never be a 'man', just a perpetual child with an insignificant voice
- I feel so unrelievably vulnerable all the time
- I believe I have less worth than a paedophile
- I can find no sense of self-love or respect in me at all and this is very frightening
- I have no sense of my own psychological needs
- My mother's happiness always comes first before mine (and by extension everyone else's)
- If I can't even 'attract' my mother, then I am ugly to all females
- I am very scared of my parents
- I deserve no rest

A massive weight and burden to carry daily

- Every day I have to 'tread water' to avoid being psychologically 'drowned' by my deep sense of shame
- Every day is a fight not to be crushed under this huge psychological burden. I am so exhausted.

HEAVY WEIGHT OF TOXIC SHAME

PULLING ME DOWN

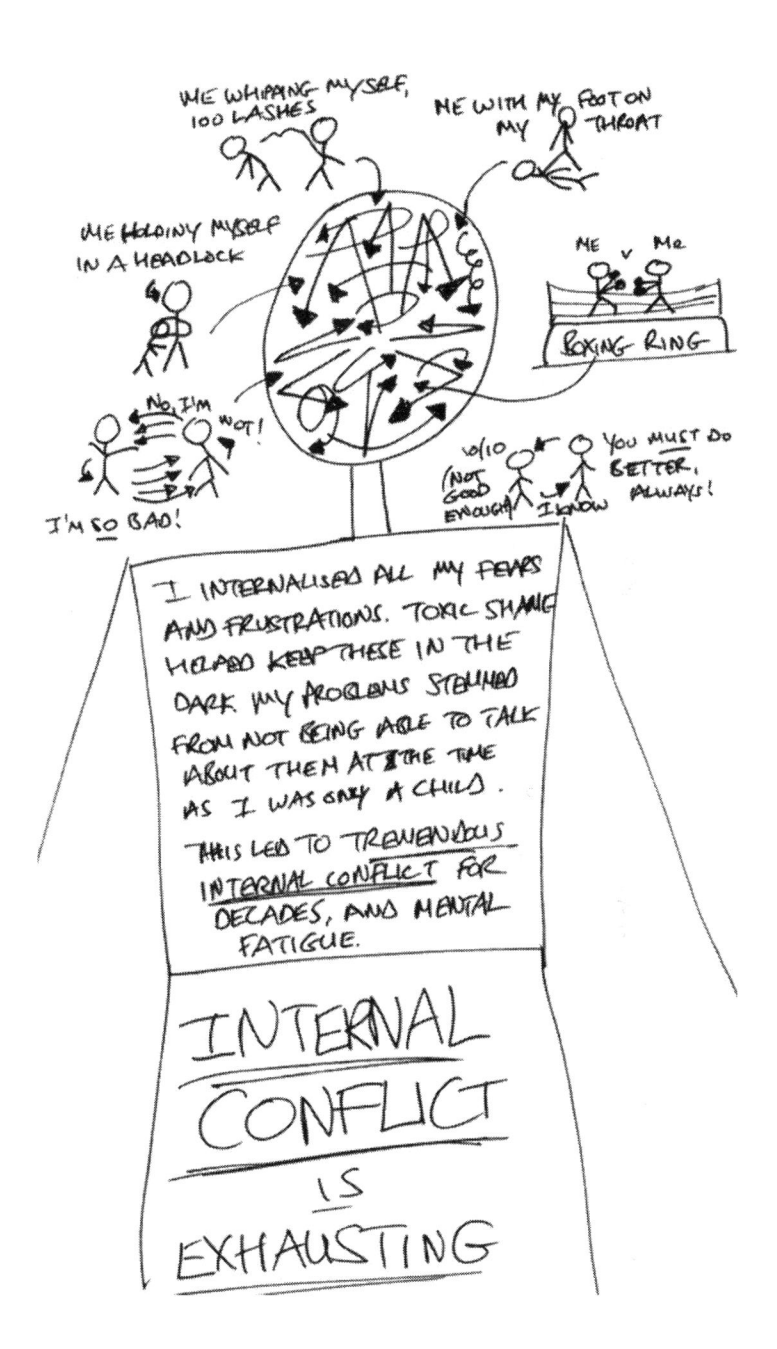

Understanding things further to fully save yourself

Me whipping myself, 100 lashes

Me with my foot on my throat

Me holding myself in a headlock

Me v Me — Boxing Ring

No, I'm not! I'm so bad!

10/10 (not good enough) I know — You must do better, always!

I internalised all my fears and frustrations. Toxic shame helped keep these in the dark. My problems stemmed from not being able to talk about them at the time as I was only a child.

This led to tremendous <u>internal conflict</u> for decades, and mental fatigue.

<u>INTERNAL CONFLICT</u> IS EXHAUSTING

> *I PUT MYSELF UNDER HUGE PSYCHOLOGICAL PRESSURE TO BE THE 'PERFECT' PERSON ALL THE TIME, PROFESSIONALLY AND SOCIALLY, TO MAKE AMENDS FOR MY 'ORIGINAL SIN' / SENSE OF TOXIC SHAME*
>
> *ME AT THE BOTTOM OF A DEEP 'OCEAN'*

I found it next to impossible ever to put myself first and look after myself emotionally. The only way I could imagine doing this was if something awful and tragic happened to me personally, then I could imagine giving myself a moment's peace of mind before reapplying pressure to myself.

> *IF, GOD FORBID, ONE OF MY CLOSE RELATIVES DIES, THEN PERHAPS I COULD PUT MYSELF FIRST, JUST FOR A FEW MINUTES, AND CARE FOR MYSELF, THAT WOULD BE SO NICE... ANY MORE THAN THAT WOULD OF COURSE BE UTTERLY SELFISH AND FAR MORE THAN I DESERVE*

Understanding things further to fully save yourself 83

I felt as if I were climbing a mental mountain every day, with disturbed, fitful sleep at nights.

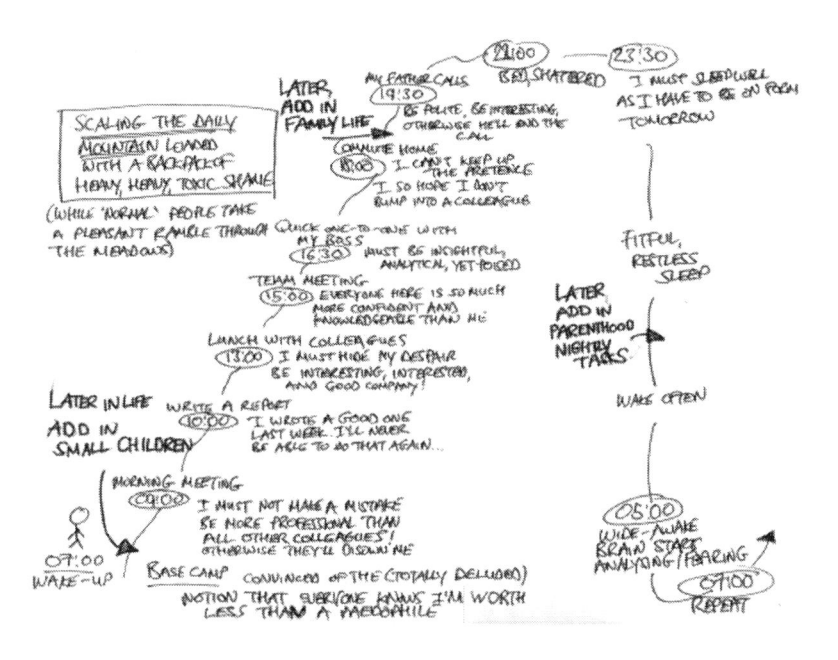

[Handwritten diagram: "SCALING THE DAILY MOUNTAIN LOADED WITH A BACKPACK OF HEAVY, HEAVY, TOXIC SHAME" (While 'normal' people take a pleasant ramble through the meadows)

Timeline from 07:00 wake-up through base camp (convinced of the (totally deluded) notion that everyone knows I'm worth less than a paedophile), 09:00 morning meeting (I must not make a mistake, be more professional than all other colleagues! otherwise they'll disown me), 10:00 write a report (I wrote a good one last week. I'll never be able to do that again...), Later in life add in small children, 13:00 lunch with colleagues (I must hide my despair, be interesting, interested, and good company!), 15:00 team meeting (everyone here is so much more confident and knowledgeable than me), 16:30 quick one-to-one with my boss (must be insightful, analytical, yet focused), Later, add in family life, 18:00 commute home (I can't keep up the pretence. I so hope I don't bump into a colleague), 19:30 my father calls (be polite, be interesting, otherwise he'll end the call), 22:00 bed, shattered, 23:30 I must sleep well as I have to be on form tomorrow, fitful, restless sleep, Later add in parenthood nightly tasks, wake often, 05:00 wide-awake brain starts analysing/fearing, 07:00 repeat]

THIS INTERNAL CONFLICT LED TO YEARS AND YEARS OF SLEEPLESS NIGHTS, PLUS SEVERE BED/NIGHT SWEATS (WATER ALMOST DRIPPING FROM THE SHEETS)

PLUS CLUMPS OF HAIR SOMETIMES FALLING OUT

(ME IN THE SHOWER, CLUMPS OF HAIR FALLING OUT)

EXCRUCIATING INSECURITY, PARANOID THOUGHTS

I had feelings of excruciating insecurity, forcing me to flee social gatherings (fight or flight). They affected every day of my life and led to all types of distorted behaviours. These powerful and often overwhelming negative feelings can be hard to convey to a 'normal' person.

I must have done <u>something</u> shameful…

> *I can't believe I did/didn't do that last night* ?!
> I would regularly wake up after a night out and immediately ask myself what shameful behaviour* I had conducted the previous night
> (* Even though I was one of the politest and most thoughtful persons around)

Paranoid shame-filled thoughts driven by confirmation bias.

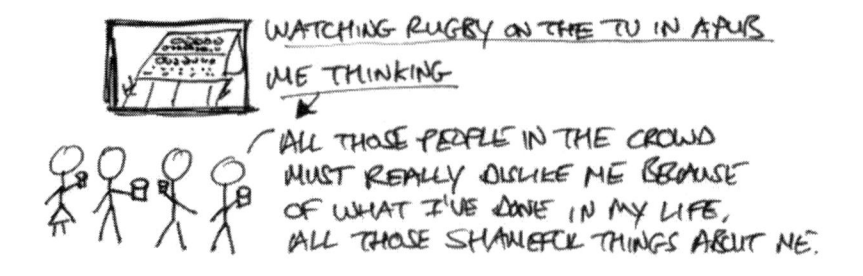

> Watching rugby on the TV in a pub
> Me thinking:
> All those people in the crowd must really dislike me because of what I've done in my life, all those shameful things about me.

Such thoughts affected my professional, working life – although I became adept at covering up and managing the stress, just about, until it all became too much for me one day. Many of us become very skilled at masking our true sense of pain. The term high-performance anxiety comes to mind in this context.

[Illustration: stick figures around a table]
NEW COLLEAGUE WHOM I'D NEVER MET BEFORE, FROM A DIFFERENT COUNTRY
ME THINKING "SHE MUST BE SO ASHAMED OF ME"
MY EXPECTATIONS OF SHAME BECAME TOTALLY DELUSIONAL

[Illustration: stick figures wearing wigs in a meeting room]
MEETING ROOM AT WORK
ME
COLLEAGUES WEARING JUDGES' WIGS
GAVEL

WHENEVER I SPOKE AT MEETINGS I FELT LIKE EVERYONE ELSE THERE WERE LIKE JUDGES, JUST WAITING FOR ME TO MAKE A MISTAKE

[Illustration: stick figure at desk]
IN WORK, FOR A PERIOD, I WOULD OFTEN BE REALLY SCARED OF MAKING LITTLE MISTAKES
CAN I JUST (TRIPLE-DOUBLE) CHECK THAT I SHOULD SEND THAT (INNOCUOUS) EMAIL NOW?
YOU MEAN THE ONE I JUST CLEARED AND SENT TO YOU MARKED "PLEASE DISTRIBUTE NOW"?

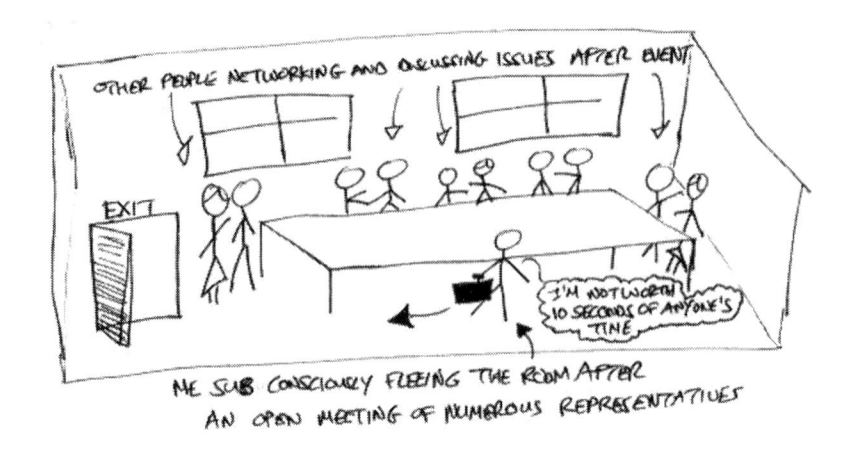

[Sketch: a meeting room with stick figures around a table. Labels: "OTHER PEOPLE NETWORKING AND DISCUSSING ISSUES AFTER EVENT", "EXIT", thought bubble "I'M NOT WORTH 10 SECONDS OF ANYONE'S TIME". Caption: "ME SUB CONSCIOUSLY FLEEING THE ROOM AFTER AN OPEN MEETING OF NUMEROUS REPRESENTATIVES"]

My mind would think up any ridiculous reason to convince itself that my colleagues were somehow better than me, because of my mind's in-built extreme (negative) confirmation bias.

[Sketch with handwritten text: "MY MIND WOULD FILL WITH NONSENSE REASONS WHY OTHER WORK COLLEAGUES WERE 'BETTER' THAN ME, THANKS TO MY CONFIRMATION BIAS". Thought bubble contents: "- THAT PERSON SPEAKS BETTER GERMAN THAN ME", "- SHE IS BETTER AT PRESENTATIONS", "- HE SOUNDS CLEVERER", "- HER FORMER WORK TITLE SOUNDS MUCH MORE PROFESSIONAL THAN ANYTHING I'VE DONE", "- HE WENT TO A BETTER SCHOOL THAN ME". Label: "09:00 WORK"]

This paranoia extended to my expecting to be fired each time my boss wanted to see me, even though I knew I was well respected as a colleague.

I felt an inordinate and distorted amount of responsibility for other people's emotional well-being.

The paranoia also extended to social drinks with old work colleagues.

[Illustration: Two stick figures at a bar table. Speech bubble: "WHY ON EARTH DOES HE WANT TO SPEND TIME WITH ME? I HAVE TO MAKE A HUGE EFFORT TO REWARD HIM FOR HIS TIME. I'M SO TIRED". Caption: "ME HAVING A DRINK WITH AN OLD FRIEND"]

This permanent sense of being submissive distorted my views of friendship.

[Illustration: A thought bubble labelled "ME SUBMITTING AND SUBORDINATING MYSELF" showing stick figures labelled "FRIENDS". Stick figure below with speech bubble: "I'VE DONE MY JOB AND PLAYED MY ROLE OF BEING VERY SUBMISSIVE AND TRYING TO ALWAYS PLEASE ALL MY FRIENDS, ESPECIALLY MY FEMALE FRIENDS. NOW THEY MUST GIVE ME LOTS OF PERSONAL ATTENTION AND PRAISE. AFTER ALL, THAT'S HOW RELATIONSHIPS WORK! I SUBMIT TO THEM AND THEY LOVE ME IN RETURN..."]

Deep down I craved love and attention. I would listen to the lyrics of Razorlight's *Wire to wire* repeatedly, especially the lines, "Love me, wherever you are/I've been looking for someone to believe in, love me, again and again/Love me, wherever you are/You've been looking for someone to believe in to love you until your eyes run dry".

SUBCONSCIOUSLY LOOKING FOR A SURROGATE MOTHER AND FATHER

My childhood experiences distorted my understanding of how my adult relationships in life would work. I assumed they would all be conditional on my playing a submissive role in order not to be abandoned.

[Diagram: Mother, Father, and God figures above a kneeling figure labelled "ME BOWING DOWN IN 'SUBMISSION' IN RETURN FOR LOVE"]

I applied this role subconsciously to my relationships, which came across on occasion as a bit weird to say the least – and as a big turn-off for women alas, which reinforced my childhood fear of not being loveable. As a result, my first and only girlfriend before I married was, with hindsight, a predictable disaster.

[Diagram: A woman and a man stick figure with the note "ME SUB-CONSCIOUSLY I MUST ALWAYS PLEASE HER, AND BE SUBMISSIVE TO HER AS I HAVE A DEEP FEAR OF BEING REPRIMANDED FOR NOT DOING SO"; "MY ONLY EVER GIRLFRIEND BEFORE MARRYING LED TO A SLOW 'CAR CRASH' OUTCOME"]

I followed my childhood script subconsciously. For more on the topic of life scripts see the section in my first book on transactional analysis, and an interesting theory about human interaction, at www.ericberne.com/transactional-analysis/

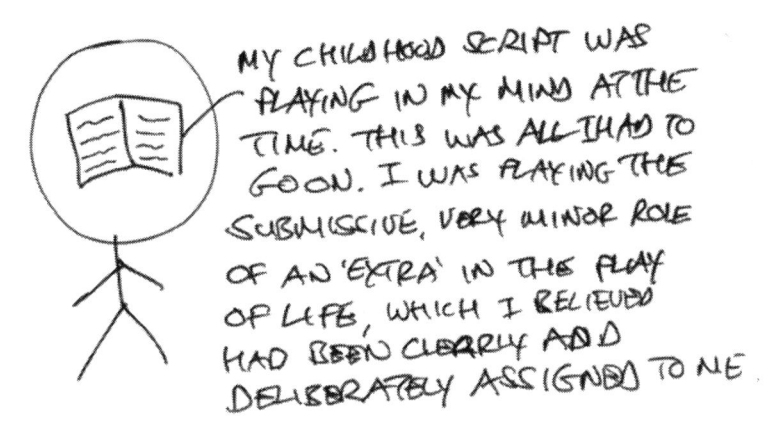

My childhood script was playing in my mind at the time. This was all I had to go on. I was playing the submissive, very minor role of an 'extra' in the play of life, which I believed had been clearly and deliberately assigned to me.

As an adult, whenever I came across an attractive woman, I not only admired her beauty, but subconsciously hoped that she might fulfil my unmet childhood need to be mothered.

An attractive woman. Me. Wow, she's so attractive but deep down I was thinking... ...could you please 'mummy me' and coddle me?

[Drawing: Adult figure labeled "ADULT ME" holding a swaddled baby, with handwritten text:] MY DESIRE, SUB-CONSCIOUSLY, WAS TO BE PAMPERED, SPOILT, INDULGED, MOLLYCODDLED, AND COSSETTED; TO HAVE SOMEONE TO TREAT ME LIKE A CHILD AGAIN, PROTECT ME AND LOOK AFTER MY EVERY NEED

I had to be very vigilant not to succumb to the temptation or desire to see my wife as a maternal figure who could 'mummy' and coddle me like an infant.

[Drawing: Two figures with a swaddled baby crossed out between them, thought bubble:] MY BEAUTIFUL WIFE IS NOT MY MOTHER

I also experienced similar distorted thinking regarding my sense of masculinity and how I saw myself in relation to other men.

UNDERSTANDING THINGS FURTHER TO FULLY SAVE YOURSELF   93

I was so desperate to be recognised and taken seriously by other men (especially my father, of course)

← Other men

Me, almost begging for attention

I would also catch myself looking for a surrogate father

"What a nice man. Will you be my daddy?"

← Random man who appeared considerate and kind to me

Drop-in "Fix it" Centre

Repair man at a "Fix-it" centre →

PHONE REPAIR

← Me

Recently I was chatting to an older man at a repair workshop. We worked together for a while trying to fix my phone and my headphones

I found myself thinking: "I'd love to stay here all day fixing things, pretending this man is my daddy."

Body dysmorphia in men is an issue that is perhaps far more prevalent among us than many people realise.

MIRROR
ME
UGH, SKINNY AND UGLY, HORRIBLE
I STILL SUFFER FROM BODY BLUES THINKING I'LL BE ATTRACTIVE WHEN I'M AS MUSCULAR AS CRISTIANO RONALDO

GROOVES, DEFCON AND ANGRY BIRDS

My childhood experiences created a deep groove of negativity in my mind which my thoughts always seemed to follow. It's a bit like an old record player stylus getting stuck in one deep groove of negative thinking without being able to move to more positive grooves elsewhere on the record/in the mind.

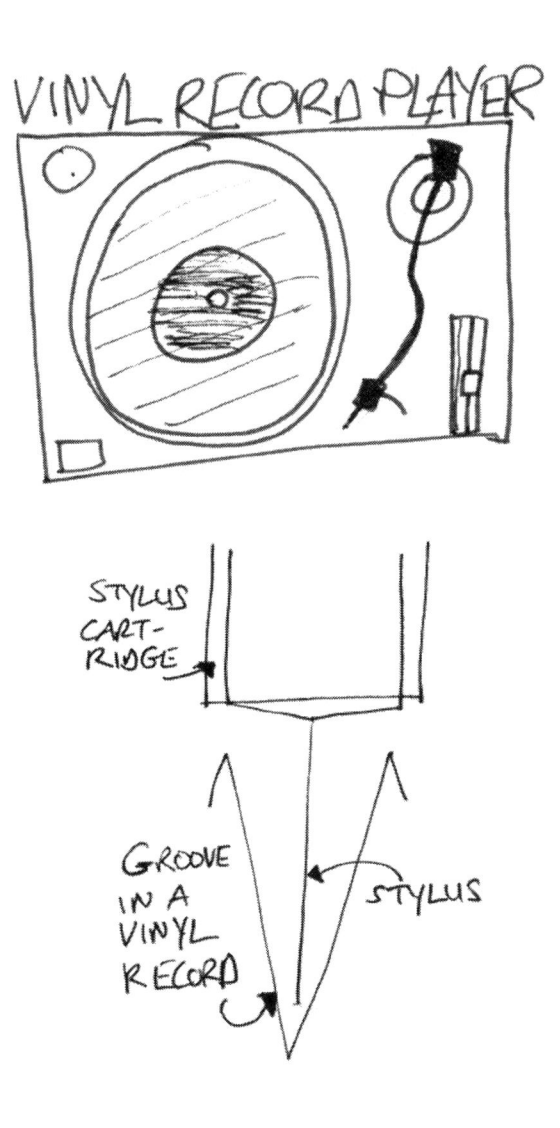

A thought always seemed to stay in this 'record groove' as it was so deep and entrenched. I was stuck in this mode of thinking until therapy, when I managed to create newer, more positive grooves in my mind for my inner stylus to follow.

Because I often felt so emotionally insecure, I was on a permanent state of alert, paranoid that I might experience again some of my childhood fears. The DEFense readiness CONdition (DEFCON) is an alert state used by the United States Armed Forces. It prescribes five graduated levels of readiness (or states of alert) that increase in severity from DEFCON 5 (least severe) to DEFCON 1 (most severe) to match varying military situations. I often felt that my brain was hardwired to be on at least DEFCON 4 most of the time.

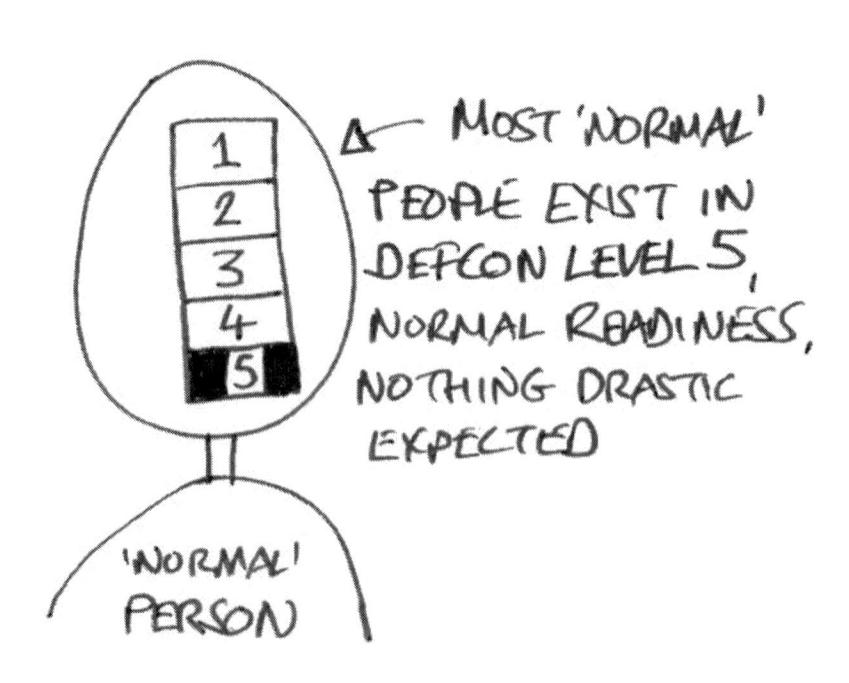

Most 'normal' people exist in DEFCON level 5, normal readiness, nothing drastic expected

'NORMAL' PERSON

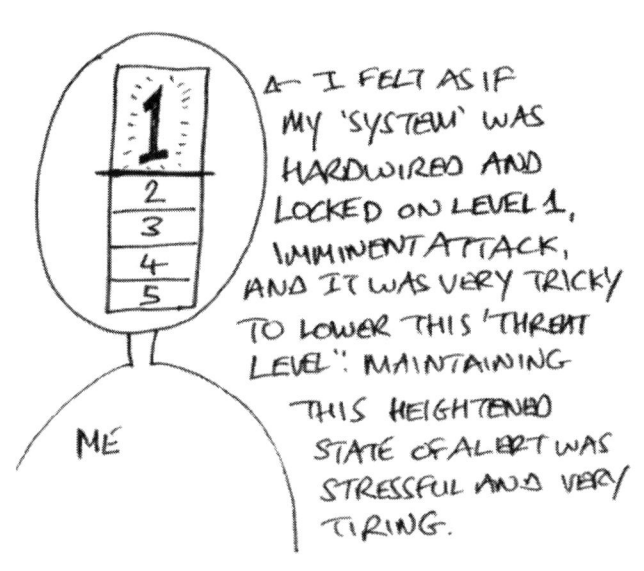

UNDERSTANDING THINGS FURTHER TO FULLY SAVE YOURSELF   97

I FELT AS IF MY 'SYSTEM' WAS HARDWIRED AND LOCKED ON LEVEL 1, IMMINENT ATTACK, AND IT WAS VERY TRICKY TO LOWER THIS 'THREAT LEVEL'. MAINTAINING THIS HEIGHTENED STATE OF ALERT WAS STRESSFUL AND VERY TIRING.

I was always in a fragile mental state, trying to accommodate my competing, and often contradictory, insecurities and fears. The smallest event could tip this precarious balance and my mind would become a restless and stormy place, resulting in weeks of poor sleep.

My mind as a precarious Angry Birds structure.

MY MIND AS A PRECARIOUS 'ANGRY BIRDS' STRUCTURE

BEFORE THERAPY MY MINDSET FELT LIKE A VERY FRAGILE AND PRECARIOUS 'ANGRY BIRDS' STRUCTURE. THE BLOCKS AND STICKS/COLUMNS REPRESENT MY MANY FEARS AND INSECURITIES OCCUPYING THE CRAMPED SPACE OF MY MIND.

IF SOME UNFORESEEN EVENT UNSETTLED ME (REPRESENTED BY THE INCOMING 'ANGRY BIRD') ALL MY UNADDRESSED FEARS AND INSECURITIES IN MY MIND FELT LIKE THEY WOULD COME CRASHING DOWN, LEAVING ME FEELING TRAUMATISED, CONFUSED AND DEPRESSED, FOLLOWED BY WEEKS OF POOR SLEEP BEFORE I REBUILT THE STRUCTURE.

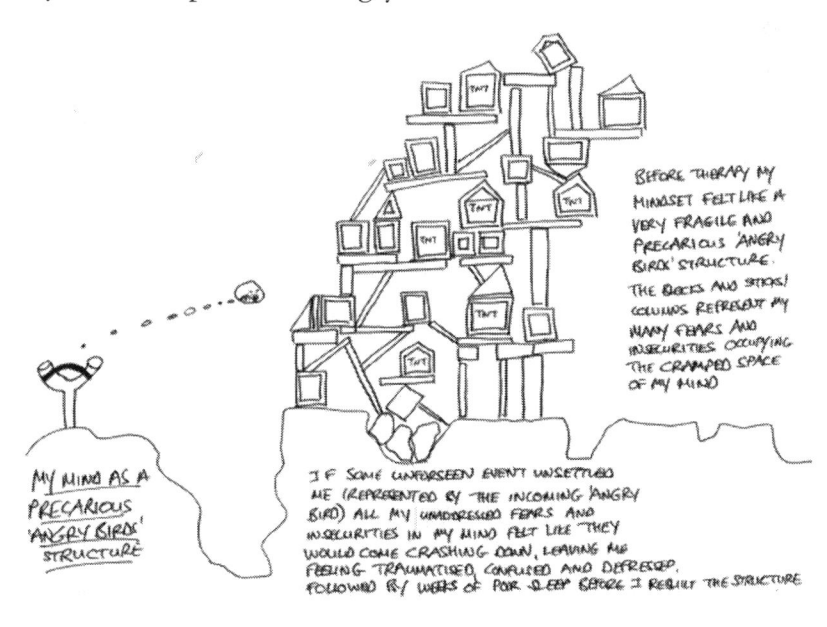

UNDERSTANDING THE IMPLICATIONS – INNER FAMILY THERAPY

"Your value doesn't decrease based on someone's inability to see your worth."

In my first book, I discussed how to free oneself by understanding how we interact with other people – based on the approach to therapy called transactional analysis, developed by Eric Berne. Here, I would like to discuss an approach called Inner Family Therapy. It is also sometimes referred to as the Internal Family Systems Model. Much of the following content is taken from the excellent resources available at www.sfhelp.org.

The concept of Inner Family Therapy believes that our personalities can be divided into Managers, Inner Kids, and Guardians – or Managers, Exiles, and Firefighters, according to the Internal Family Systems Model, founded by Dr. Richard Schwartz. I found it very useful to try and identify my traits within each of these three parts of my personality. All these sub-selves have the same goal: to look after you as well as possible. However, they all have to get to know each other and trust and rely on each other.

A well-functioning, mentally healthy person has his/her distinct parts meshing together harmoniously like the almost invincible New Zealand All Blacks rugby team. Whereas my personality before therapy was like a team of players who had never met before, spoke different languages, didn't know the rules, and often weren't even aware they were in the same team. The aim is for you to get to know your team's players, make sure they get to know each other, and get them all pulling in the same direction. If you manage to achieve some of this, you will feel much more unified as a person.

Once I had identified my traits, or subselves, I went to a quiet place, closed my eyes, and tried to connect with these distinct parts of me. Once I felt I had connected with them I spoke to them in diverse ways, depending on the trait. For example, I tried to be very gentle and to console the abandoned, sad and shamed inner kid within me, reassuring him that he was in a safe place and could relax at long last. I recommend you give it a go!

Common Personality Sub-Selves

Manager
True Self (leader)
Spiritual One/s
Organiser/Planner
Striver/Achiever
Adult ("common sense")
Historian ("memory")
Observer/Reporter
Wise One (Sage/Crone)
Nurturer
Health director
Analyser/Thinker
Creative One/Artist
Explorer/Learner

Inner Kid
Abandoned
Angry/Rageful
Curious
Good (obedient)
Guilty
Innocent /Naive
Loving
Lost/Orphan
Lusty Teen
Playful/Social
Rebellious
Sad/Hopeless
Scared
Shamed

Guardian
Blocker/Doubter
Comforter/Addict
Competitor/Aggressor
Critic/Judge/Preacher
Catastrophiser
Fantasiser/Idealist-Optimist
Magician/Distracter
Manipulator/Controller
Number/Anaesthetist
Procrastinator
Pleaser/Entertainer
Perfectionist
Saboteur/Troublemaker

PART 2
SAVING YOURSELF

This anonymous quote encapsulates many of my problems: "Fundamentally, it's not what happened to you, but your inability to talk about it at the time". Finding someone to talk to in an honest and professional manner is fundamental and a sign of real courage. Taking this first step is half the battle. Prior to seeking help, the mental maze I had been left in as a young child became more psychologically complex after marriage and having our first child. In a close relationship with emotional demands it's almost impossible to repress your fears and insecurities and to mentally hide away from everything. I felt I had plunged back into the middle of my mental maze, feeling more emotionally lost, scared and lonely than ever.

Attending numerous sessions with a psychotherapist, undertaking so-called talking therapy, helped me to pinpoint where I was in the maze, and then gave me a mental 'stepladder' which allowed me to see the layout of the remainder of the maze between me and the exit.

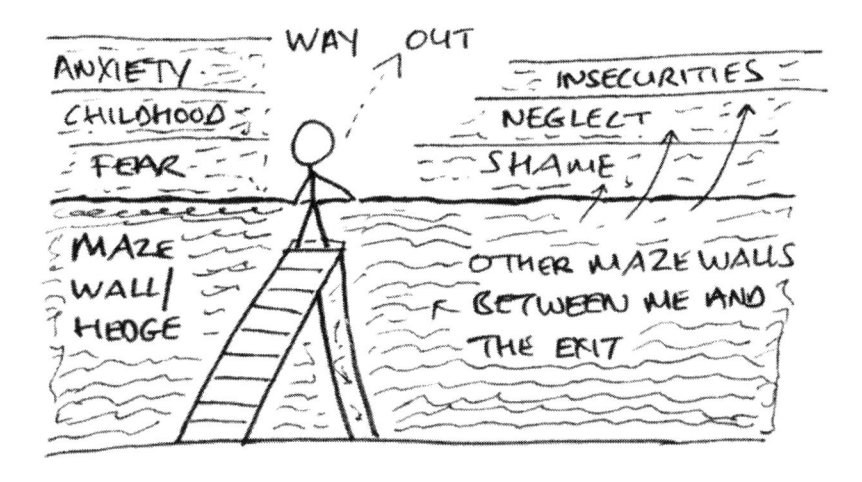

I took brief notes after each therapy session to remind myself what we had discussed and any notable developments or personal revelations that I had found particularly helpful. I would add to these notes whenever I felt pangs of insecurity, which was often; writing down what I was feeling during these emotionally fragile episodes helped me to understand more about what I was going through; just seeing my thoughts in black and white was very helpful. I was able to use this growing list of notes as a kind of 'emotional sat-nav' to find my way out.

CHALLENGING YOUR ASSUMPTIONS AND FACING YOUR FEARS

Challenging your assumptions and facing your fears involves interrogating yourself to get to the truth. This broadly involves asking yourself the following:

- Have I ever challenged, and challenged again, *all* my assumptions about how I see myself? No, never; it never even occurred to me. I just assumed this is how I am and that's it
- How do I really, deep down, value and see myself as a person? Um, now you ask, OK, I think…
- Answer the same question again with brutal honesty after some real self-reflection. OK, in my case, less than humanly possible; know what infinity is? Well in terms of poor self-regard, go past it and keep going…
- Why do I believe this? Not sure when I think about it…
- What evidence is there? Well, it's always been like that, I've never known any different and it's engrained in my every fibre of being
- Does evidence exist? OK, if I really think about it, it's circumstantial at best, only my interpretations of other/my parents' behaviour
- When did I come to these beliefs? When I was a scared, egocentric infant with an underdeveloped brain and no ego defences
- Could I have been wrong therefore? Absolutely, 100% yes
- If I am wrong about everything I know about myself, then what is the truth about me? I'm going to find out and I'm excited about the prospects
- So, if I challenge all my assumptions, I will find my authentic self again? Absolutely, yes, and what a reward that is.

Your fears want to be confronted.

My experience is that your fears want you to confront and overcome them. They are on your side. You just must find the courage to confront and comfort these cornered animals and they will respond eventually with endless gratitude and relief. Only then can you stand tall and be the authentic you that the world needs.

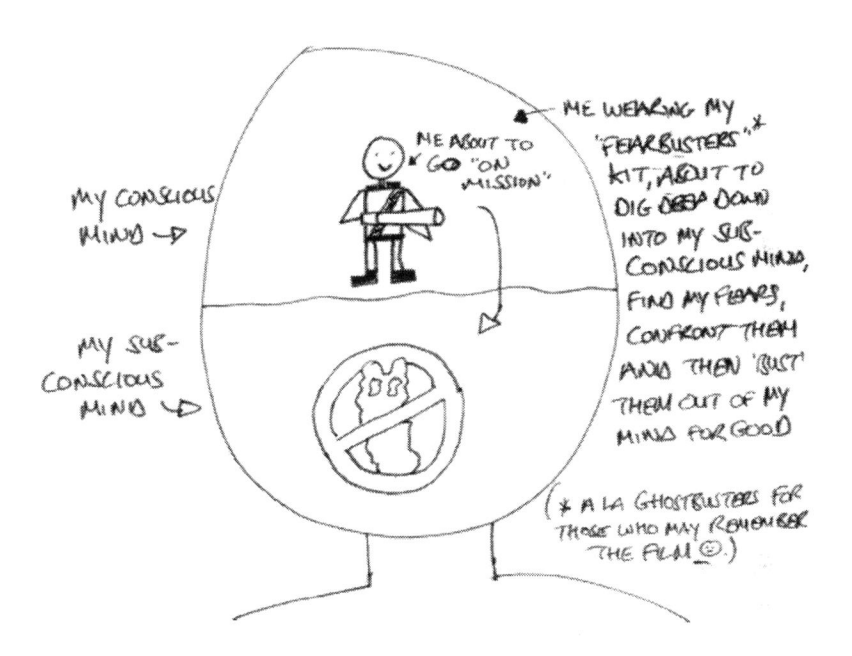

To do this, I would try to go to the most frightening places in my mind, which I had abandoned in childhood, and remain there to challenge my inner demons until I could reclaim these parts of my mind as peaceful, calm and confident places. I also did this with recurring nightmares I had been having. I would dream that I was being held hostage in our old family home by an evil, merciless man standing in the enclosed garden. It was frightening to imagine confronting this evil man; however, after some effort I progressed from just looking at him through a window to thinking about confronting him, to going out and doing so, to telling him I wasn't scared and that he was a figment of my imagination, and to facing him down until the fear dissipated. Finally, I imagined inviting him into the house and opening the door for him to enter. I told him he could roam around inside the house and to stay as long as he wanted. Eventually, I felt him transform from a menacing, evil person to a subdued, passive, unthreatening, kindly person who had been though trauma and only wanted a long, uninterrupted rest.

I had recurring dreams of being alone as a child in my family home with a very menacing strange man outside in the garden who had total control over me and my access into and out of the house.

The dreams only stopped when I had the courage to imagine myself confronting this threatening person.

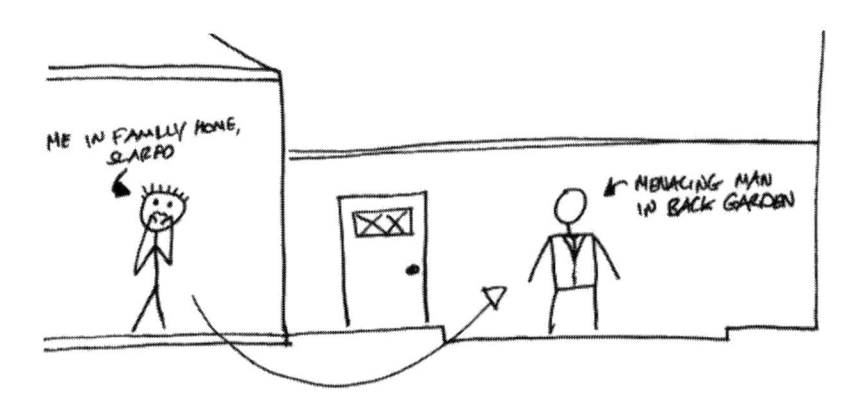

Firstly, I imagined myself confronting him (which was rather frightening), then telling him I'm not scared of him and, overtime, eventually showing I was in charge by inviting him into the house. And then, finally, I imagined myself embracing him, telling him I know he is in fact the one who is scared and telling him to use the house as long as he needed to relax and find peace of mind. I remember a part of me feeling really relieved inside, and grateful.

BLACK IS WHITE AND VICE VERSA

When you start to realise that everything you assumed about your value as a human being is wrong, it's like suddenly telling yourself what you always thought was black is in fact white and vice versa. It goes against all you've assumed to be 100% true.

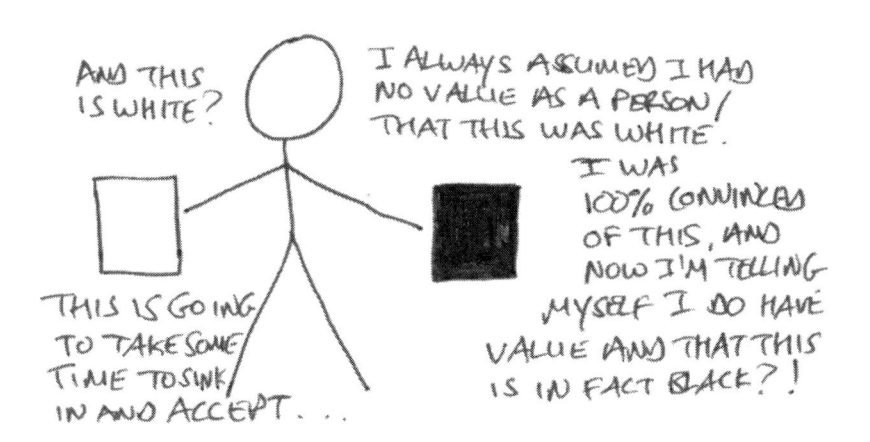

AND THIS IS WHITE?

THIS IS GOING TO TAKE SOME TIME TO SINK IN AND ACCEPT...

I ALWAYS ASSUMED I HAD NO VALUE AS A PERSON / THAT THIS WAS WHITE. I WAS 100% CONVINCED OF THIS, AND NOW I'M TELLING MYSELF I DO HAVE VALUE AND THAT THIS IS IN FACT BLACK?!

You need courage to allow yourself to believe what seems a ridiculous notion, but which is in fact completely true. It is unsettling, like feeling a small earthquake under your feet for the first time. However, keep the faith and each day you will recognise the truth of what at first seemed an absurd claim.

OVERCOMING WRONGFUL (EMOTIONAL) CONVICTION

A prime goal is realising that you are innocent of the convictions that originated in your childhood. A prisoner wrongly convicted at least knows he was wronged. That's not the case for children who assume they are guilty of being fundamentally deficient before they are able to understand what is happening to them. It's as if they have been convicted in secret and the ruling thrown away. If no one is aware of a childhood 'conviction' forty years in the past, if even the defendant doesn't know, and there is no evidence of any charges or sentencing, then how can exoneration occur?

Getting some form of 'appeal' together takes courage and tenacity. First you need to realise that something untoward happened to you earlier in your life. Then you need courage to investigate the case, without being sure of any success, and the tenacity to keep going when others may doubt your purpose. You may even have to present evidence to the people who 'convicted' you unwittingly (parents mostly) who have absolutely no recollection or idea that they ever did so in the first place. It can be a lonely struggle, but eventually the truth will materialise, and you will find deeper respect for yourself on the path to exoneration.

How I viewed my 'conviction' as a child.

IN MY EYES

"JUDGE" — YOU ARE GUILTY OF NOT BEING GOOD ENOUGH EVEN FOR YOUR OWN PARENTS!

ME

THE JUDGE (A COMBINATION OF BOTH MY PARENTS) HAD COME TO A CLEAR VERDICT

I jailed my real, authentic self within my mind to carry out the 'sentence passed down on me'. Because of my shame and weak ego, I believed I did not have the authority to release my real self from this self-imposed prison and that the only people who could do so were my parents.

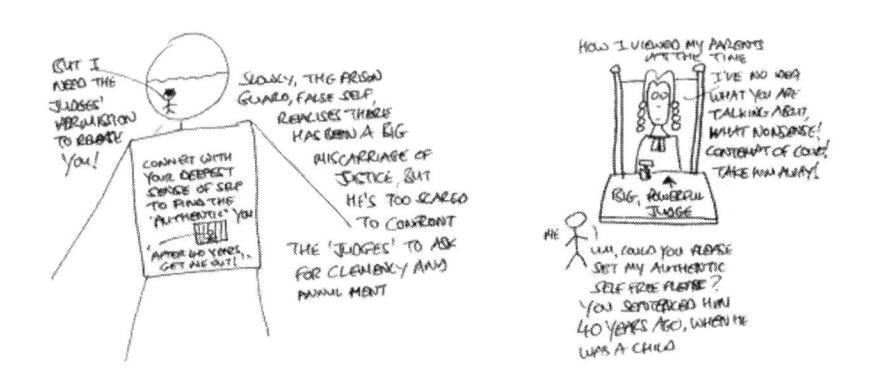

To free myself from jail I first had to convince myself that an injustice towards me had possibly been committed.

[Sketch: "POSITIVE LIGHT" shining on two stick figures labelled "MY PARENTS" and a smaller figure labelled "ME". Caption: "THIS IS DIFFICULT AT FIRST AS WE ALL HAVE A TENDENCY TO VIEW OUR PARENTS WEARING 'ROSE-TINTED' GLASSES"]

Once you overcome this, you need to find your case file; long ago forgotten about and discarded (especially as one's parents very often don't even realise they had sentenced you).

My parents, here represented by the judge, were not even aware that they had 'convicted' me, so appealing to them was no good.

[Sketch: "HOW I VIEWED MY PARENTS AT THE TIME" — a "BIG, POWERFUL JUDGE" saying "I'VE NO IDEA WHAT YOU ARE TALKING ABOUT, WHAT NONSENSE! CONTEMPT OF COURT! TAKE HIM AWAY!" and a small stick figure labelled "ME" saying "UM, COULD YOU PLEASE SET MY AUTHENTIC SELF FREE PLEASE? YOU SENTENCED HIM 40 YEARS AGO, WHEN HE WAS A CHILD"]

Saving Yourself

The only thing for me to do was to appeal to the 'Supreme Court' in a conceptual sense, representing reason and truth.

APPEAL! OVER THE 'JUDGES'

TO REASON AND TRUTH

I THOUGHT LONG AND HARD MENTALLY TO COME UP WITH VERY GOOD ARGUMENTS TO OVERCOME MY SENSE OF SHAME.

I further investigated my case, reading a lot about psychology, some philosophy and criticism of religion and came up with overwhelming evidence that there had been a miscarriage of justice. The 'Supreme Court' of truth and reason that I had established in my mind provided me with the authority and reason to overturn the existing conviction and free myself.

EVENTUALLY MY SENSE OF REASON AND TRUTH PREVAILED

I'M FREE!

AND I SET MYSELF FREE WITHOUT NEEDING MY PARENTS' PERMISSION

During my investigation and appeal to the 'Supreme Court' I gradually saw the truth revealing itself and caught tentative glimpses of my real self becoming free.

The following drawing depicts freeing one's authentic self from behind the fortified, thick and very strong brick wall you built around it.

At the beginning you feel tiny in front of this seemingly huge edifice. No way around. During your recovery process you'll see tantalising glimpses of your authentic, real self which will feel liberating and exciting. No way around.

Later in the progress you'll feel much bigger and stronger, able to dismantle the wall much easier.

Afterwards, my real, authentic self merged with my false self and eventually I took full control of who I really am.

Eventually your authentic self will merge with your false self = producing a unified, confident, truly and fully authentic you, full of pride, self-love, wisdom, emotional intelligence, liberated from the past and excited about the future.

A BRIEF PEP TALK

> IT WASN'T YOUR FAULT
>
> IT DIDN'T HAPPEN LIKE YOU THINK IT DID
>
> YOU ARE NOT TO BLAME
>
> IF YOU'VE COME THIS FAR... YOU ARE NO DOUBT A VERY GOOD PERSON

Unfortunately, despite much progress, many men still do not open up enough emotionally to people close to us, often out of fear of mockery.

> FOR MEN, TALKING ABOUT THEIR FEELINGS IS DIFFICULT AND SOMETIMES FRIGHTENING — THAT'S WHY ONLY <u>BRAVE</u> MEN DO IT...

Try not to compare yourself to others.

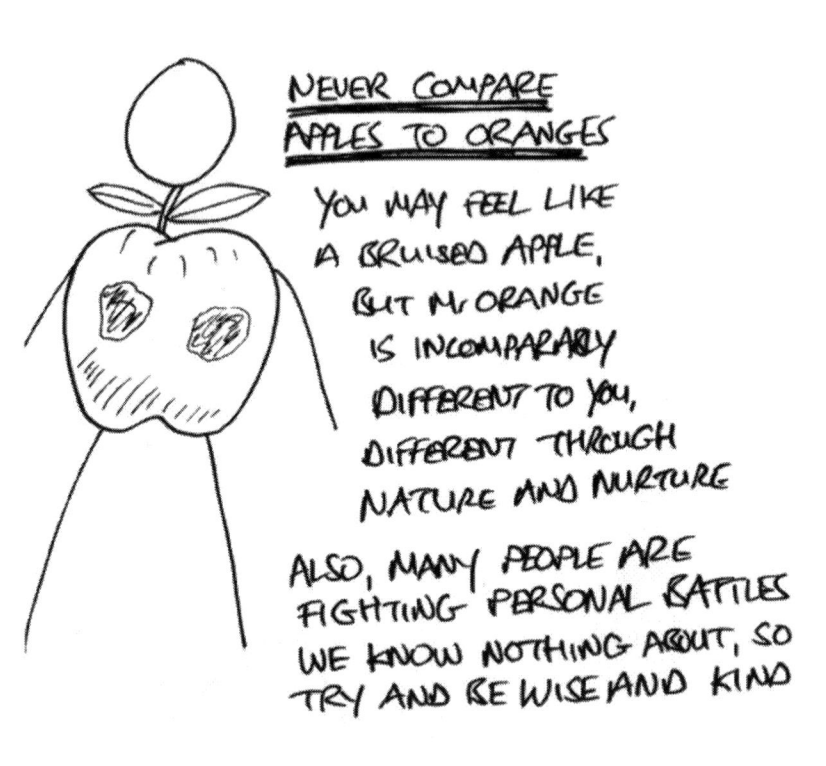

NEVER COMPARE APPLES TO ORANGES

YOU MAY FEEL LIKE A BRUISED APPLE, BUT Mr ORANGE IS INCOMPARABLY DIFFERENT TO YOU, DIFFERENT THROUGH NATURE AND NURTURE

ALSO, MANY PEOPLE ARE FIGHTING PERSONAL BATTLES WE KNOW NOTHING ABOUT, SO TRY AND BE WISE AND KIND

Mr ORANGE MAY APPEAR HEALTHIER AND BRIGHTER, BUT HE PROBABLY HAD MUCH MORE 'SUN' IN HIS LIFE GROWING UP AND DIDN'T FALL FROM THE 'FAMILY' TREE AS EARLY AND FROM SUCH A GREAT HEIGHT AS YOU.

YOU ARE PROBABLY MUCH MORE RESOURCEFUL AND RESILIENT, AND WISE THAN HE WILL EVER BE, EVEN IF YOU DON'T REALISE THIS YET.

I read a lot about my old religion of Christianity and all its claims, doctrines, history, and beliefs and I came to the firm conclusion that its supernatural claims simply do not stand up to effective criticism.

I also realised that the idea of being born 'in sin' and being regularly reminded of your 'sins' is a recipe for a sense of perpetual inadequacy. It is much better to regard oneself with pride as an amazing primate stemming from four billion years of gradual evolution than a lowly failure of a sinner.

In short, question everything, read widely, challenge claimed religious authority and supernatural claims, and work things out for yourself as an inquisitive journalist would researching a big story. If God exists, and an individual's pursuit of knowledge offends him, then he doesn't seem all that mighty to me.

OVERCOMING TOXIC SHAME

One problem I encountered was that of trying too hard to overcome my issues to become a thoroughly confident person – which turned out to be asking too much from the process. I remember one day watching an interview with the Spanish golfer Sergio Garcia, who had won a major tournament after many years of failing to do so, despite being one of the most talented golfers of his generation. He explained that he had simply accepted that winning such a title may never happen, and if this was to be the case, then he could live with this and himself. This admission of a possible painful realisation no doubt played a large part in his subsequent success by relaxing him considerably. I admitted to myself later that day that my debilitating sense of toxic shame might last until the day I die and that I would be comfortable with this if so. Since accepting this possibility my sense of shame has dwindled significantly, partly I guess because I am no longer fixated on 'fixing it'.

Shame is passed down from one generation to the next until someone says enough and deals with it. I imagined my mother handing me down this generational shame in the form of a rugby ball.

Kick away the rugby ball of shame given to you.

I imagined myself kicking this ball away immediately, never to be seen again (a bit like the British comedian Peter Kay did in his football training advert for John Smith's beer, for those of you familiar with it).

Truly ridding yourself of toxic shame involves cutting all your distorted emotional ties with your parents and then re-establishing them in a healthy manner on your terms.

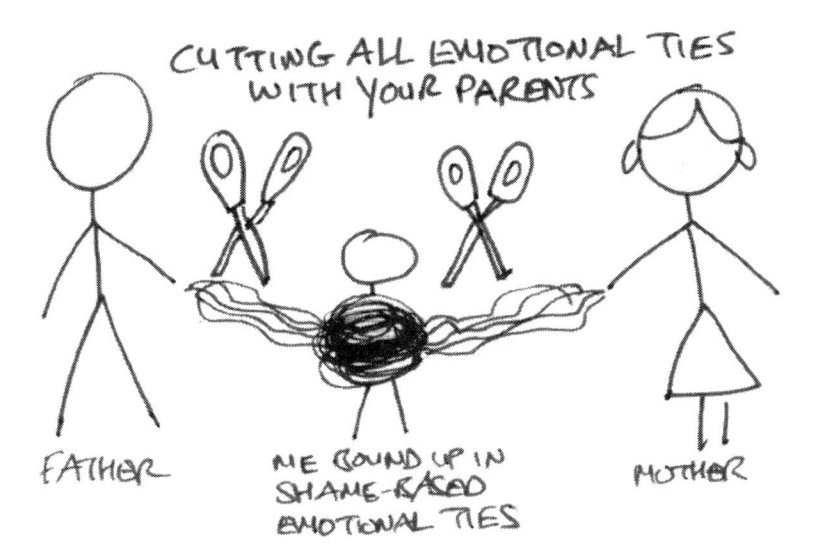

AND THEN RE-ESTABLISHING THE EMOTIONAL TIES ON YOUR TERMS, BASED ON YOUR SELF-RESPECT

Shame thrives in darkness and silence.

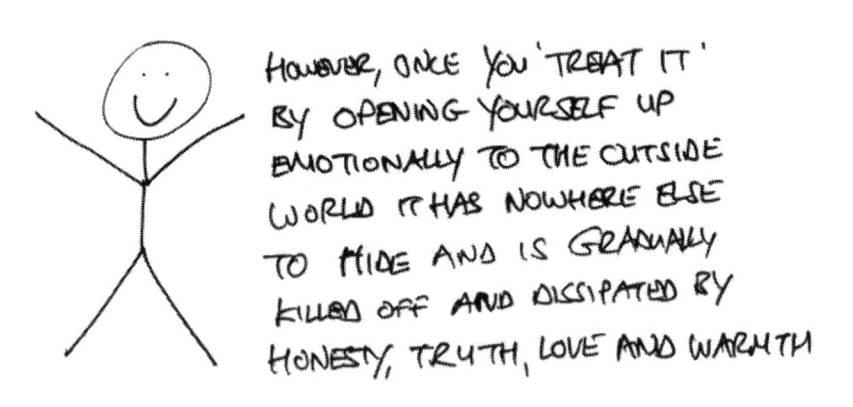

HOWEVER, ONCE YOU 'TREAT IT' BY OPENING YOURSELF UP EMOTIONALLY TO THE OUTSIDE WORLD IT HAS NOWHERE ELSE TO HIDE AND IS GRADUALLY KILLED OFF AND DISSIPATED BY HONESTY, TRUTH, LOVE AND WARMTH

Eventually, an alien concept occurred to me.

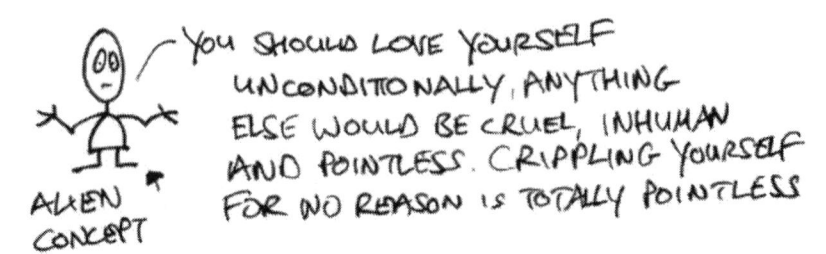

ALIEN CONCEPT — YOU SHOULD LOVE YOURSELF UNCONDITIONALLY, ANYTHING ELSE WOULD BE CRUEL, INHUMAN AND POINTLESS. CRIPPLING YOURSELF FOR NO REASON IS TOTALLY POINTLESS

!?!? THIS SEEMED SIMULTANEOUSLY THE MOST LIBERATING AND CONFUSING IDEA I HAD HAD FOR A LONG TIME. "THIS GOES AGAINST ALL MY COMMON SENSE, YET IT FEELS SOMEHOW TANTALISINGLY NICE

? "HMM, BUT IT FEELS LIKE A VERY SELFISH, ARROGANT AND VAIN THING TO DO. I FEEL VERY UNCOMFORTABLE JUST CONSIDERING IT. I'VE NEVER TAKEN MYSELF SERIOUSLY BEFORE. SOD IT, I'M JUST GOING TO TRY."

THIS FEELS WEIRD — IT'S LIKE GOING OUT IN LOVELY, SMART NEW CLOTHES FOR THE FIRST TIME, AFTER YEARS IN SCRUFFY, UNKEMPT, OLD CLOTHES. YOU FEEL VERY SELF-CONSCIOUS AND CONSPICUOUS. AFTER A WHILE THOUGH THE 'NEW CLOTHES' START TO FEEL MORE COMFORTABLE AND NATURAL

This is how I saw myself in comparison with the adults from my childhood.

Before therapy I saw all the adults in my life as giants- brave, confident and domineering people.

ADULTS IN MY LIFE WHEN I WAS A CHILD
BIG MOUNTAINS
ME AS A CHILD

After realising what an effort I was making to confront my own fears (in contrast to others), I could further deconstruct my distorted view of my parents and to finally construct a positive image of myself.

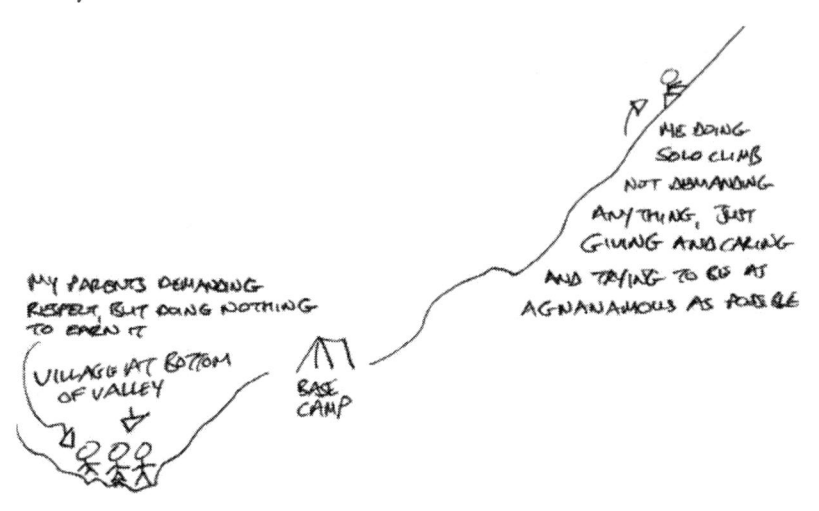

ME DOING SOLO CLIMB NOT DEMANDING ANYTHING, JUST GIVING AND CARING AND TRYING TO BE AS AGNANAMOUS AS POSSIBLE

MY PARENTS DEMANDING RESPECT, BUT DOING NOTHING TO EARN IT

VILLAGE AT BOTTOM OF VALLEY

BASE CAMP

And this is how I saw them after therapy and my recovery process.

BIG MOUNTAIN

ME SEEING PEOPLE WITH FRESH EYES AFTER THERAPY

AFTER THERAPY I REALISED THAT MANY OF THESE 'GIANTS' FROM MY CHILDHOOD ARE ACTUALLY MORE SCARED OF LIFE THAN I AM NOW

I have gone from being a frightened, insecure person with the meekness of a small mouse to a confident, good person.

BE WARY – FALLING INTO BURNOUT AND DEPRESSION

In my first book, I described my fall into burnout and depression because of the long-term psychological pressure I was under. I would like to describe in more detail here what that experience felt like. I recognise of course that these are complex, multi-faceted medical and psychological issues, hence my focus only on how it felt to me personally.

What burnout really feels like.

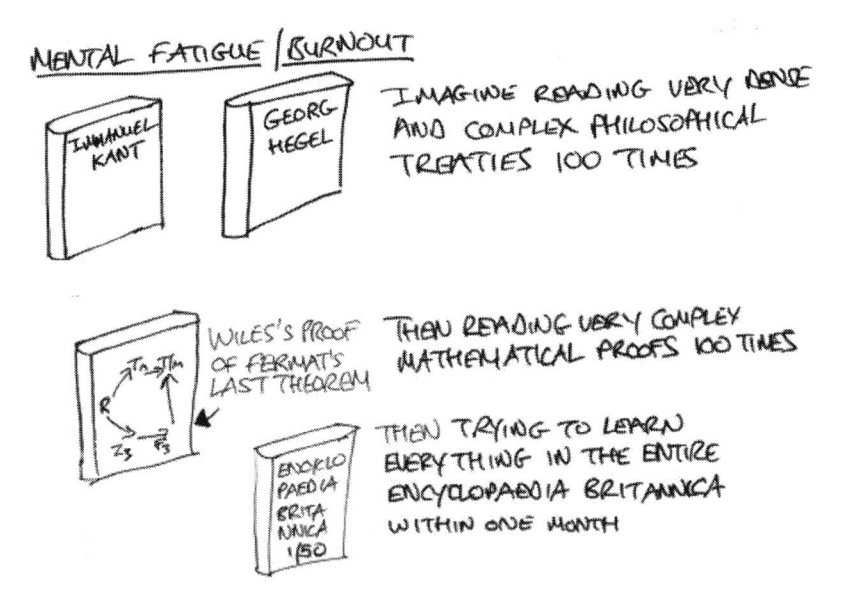

Mental fatigue / burnout: Imagine reading very dense and complex philosophical treatises 100 times (Immanuel Kant, Georg Hegel). Then reading very complex mathematical proofs 100 times (Wiles's proof of Fermat's Last Theorem). Then trying to learn everything in the entire Encyclopaedia Britannica within one month.

And then keep this going for years on end, punctuated by hundreds of nights of poor and broken sleep.

Until your brain shuts down to protect itself from damage. Shop shutter slamming down. System crash — switch off computer.

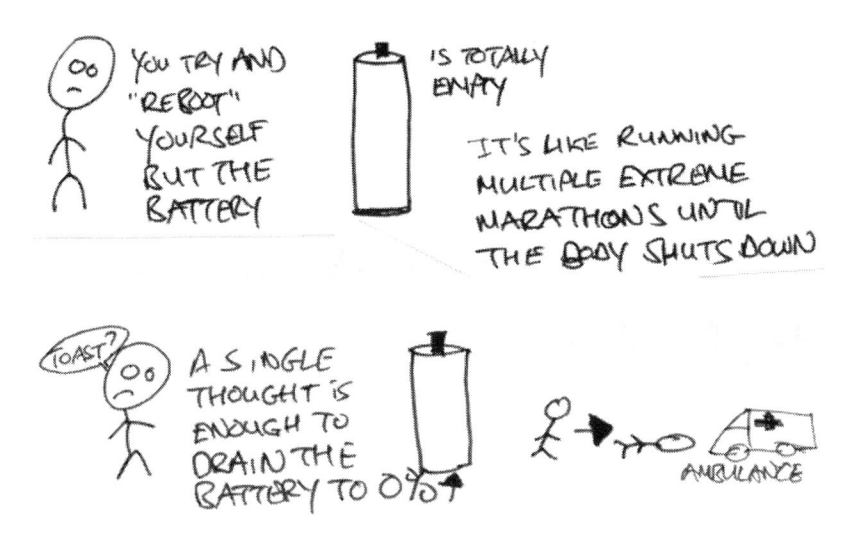

You try and "reboot" yourself but the battery is totally empty. It's like running multiple extreme marathons until the body shuts down.

(Toast?) A single thought is enough to drain the battery to 0%.

Ambulance

The brain feels like any other muscle in the body. If one does far too much exercise without properly looking after yourself, your muscles ache for some time. If you maintain the same level of exertion, something will have to give, and you may face long-term problems. My brain feels like that when I am burnt out. This ever present 'brain ache' is very unpleasant. Small thoughts popping into your mind can cause it to ache that little bit more.

Burnout is like having your head in a vice.

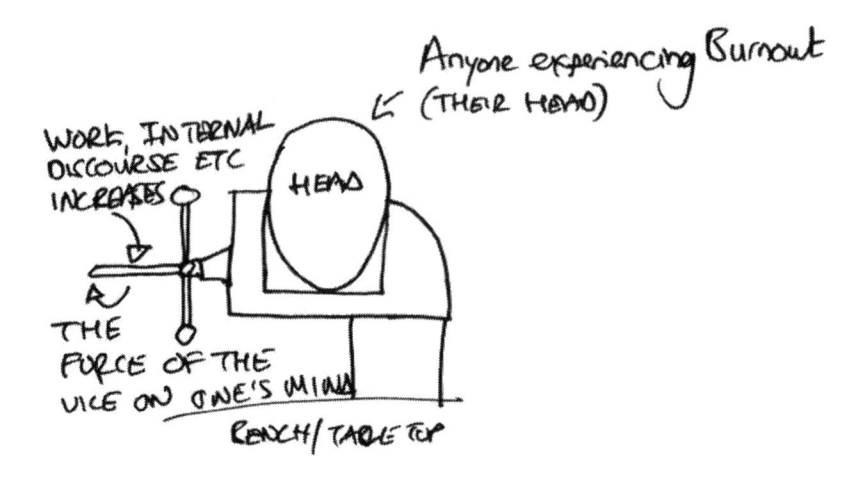

[Diagram: a head in a vice labelled "Anyone experiencing Burnout (THEIR HEAD)", with arrows showing "WORK, INTERNAL DISCOURSE ETC INCREASES" and "THE FORCE OF THE VICE ON ONE'S MIND" pressing down on the head which rests on a "BENCH/TABLE TOP".]

Alcohol weakens this vice for a short period, but makes the vice tighter in the medium to long term. However, sometimes this momentary relief is very hard to refuse.

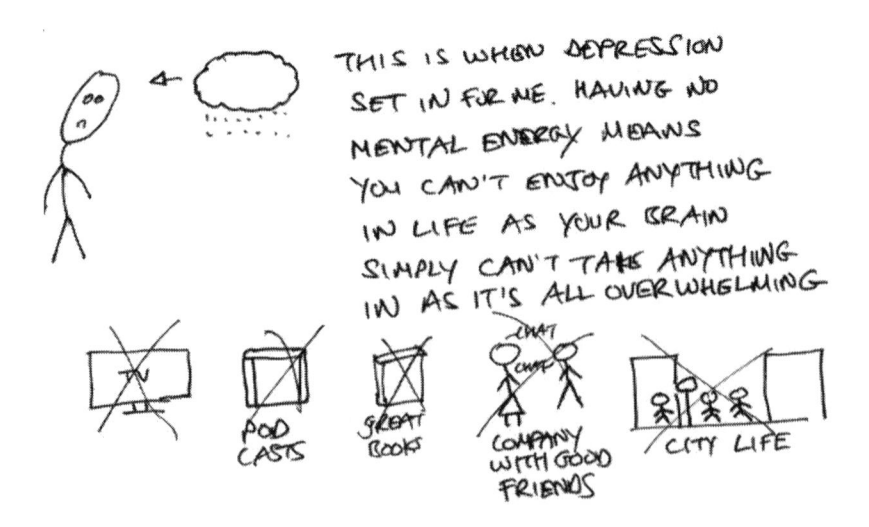

[Diagram: a stick figure with a thought cloud, captioned "THIS IS WHEN DEPRESSION SET IN FOR ME. HAVING NO MENTAL ENERGY MEANS YOU CAN'T ENJOY ANYTHING IN LIFE AS YOUR BRAIN SIMPLY CAN'T TAKE ANYTHING IN AS IT'S ALL OVERWHELMING". Below are four crossed-out icons labelled "TV", "PODCASTS", "GREAT BOOKS", "COMPANY WITH GOOD FRIENDS", and "CITY LIFE".]

Chart depicting one's ability to function normally, feel optimistic, enjoy life etc.

100%

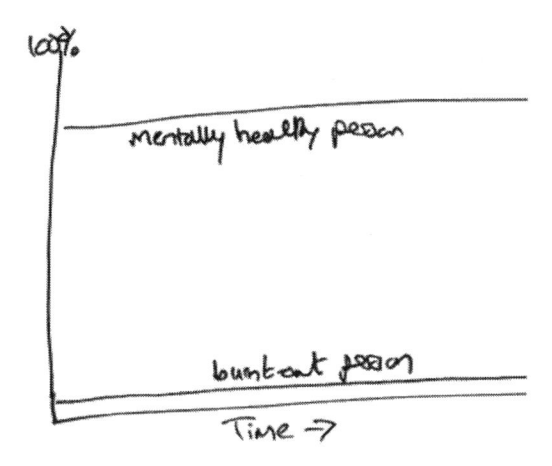

mentally healthy person

burnt-out person

Time →

Feeling like this for prolonged periods of time is very unpleasant and very frustrating.

THIS IS WHY ALCOHOL IS SO TEMPTING WHEN BURNTOUT...

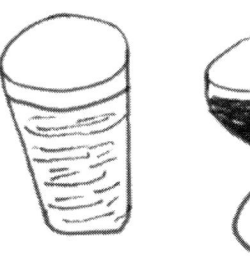

IT LIFTS YOUR SPIRITS FOR A FEW HOURS AND MAKES YOU FEEL HALFWAY NORMAL AGAIN

This is my road to burnout.

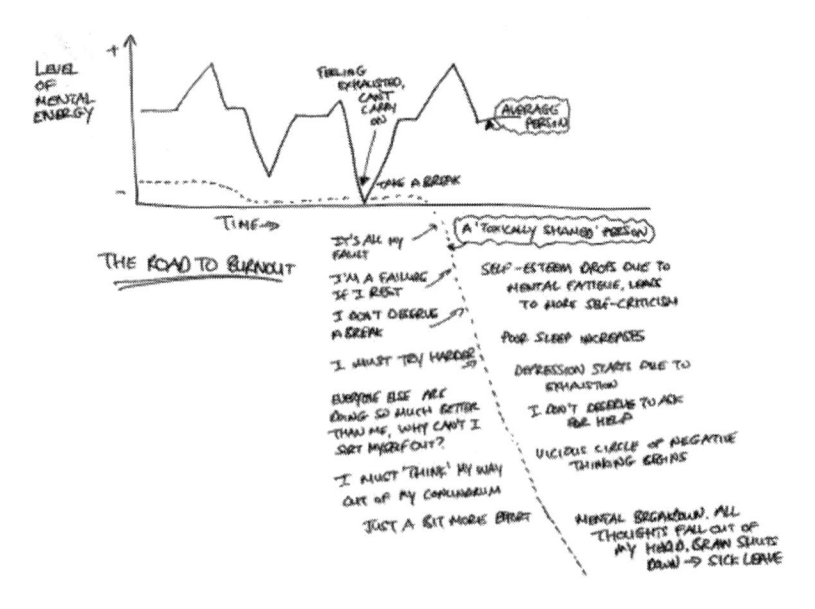

Often, it's easier not to address the obvious fact that you need to change something in your life, perhaps quite considerably.

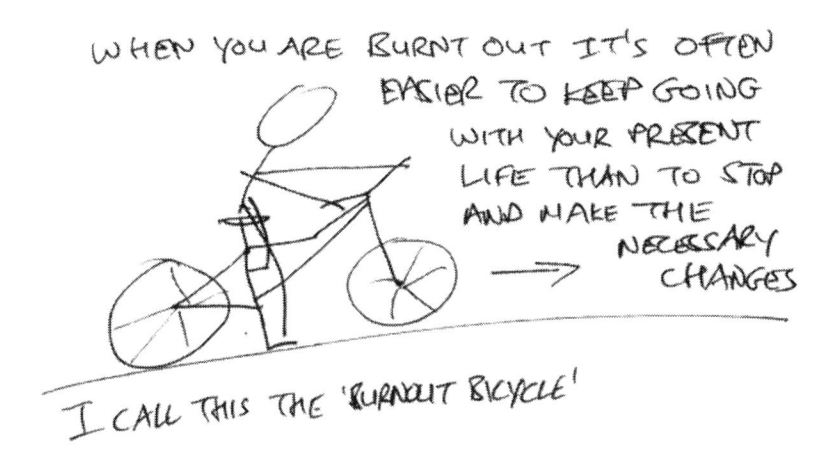

When you are burnt out it's often easier to keep going with your present life than to stop and make the necessary changes

I call this the 'Burnout Bicycle'

Getting off the burnout bicycle and reorienting yourself takes courage and effort, but it is vital to prevent the situation worsening.

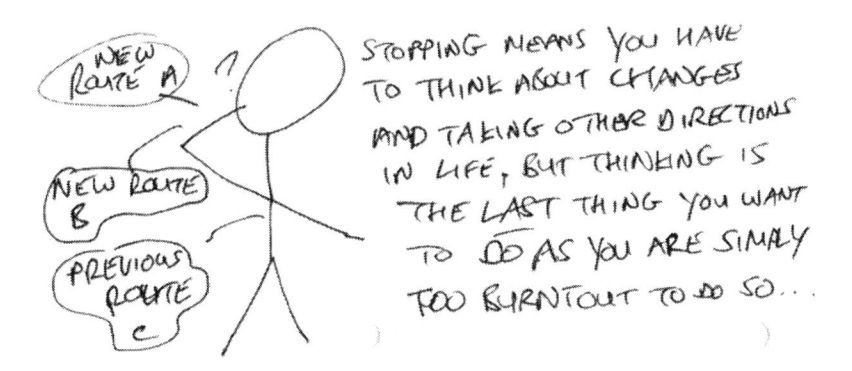

New Route A? New Route B Previous Route C

Stopping means you have to think about changes and taking other directions in life, but thinking is the last thing you want to do as you are simply too burntout to do so...

In my first book, I mentioned that one day, after weeks of poor sleep and feeling totally exhausted, all the thoughts in my mind felt as if they suddenly fell out of my mind. I'd like to expand a bit on this here and talk about what happened in the run up to this mental breakdown and how I managed to snap out of it.

128   How to Sort Your Head Out

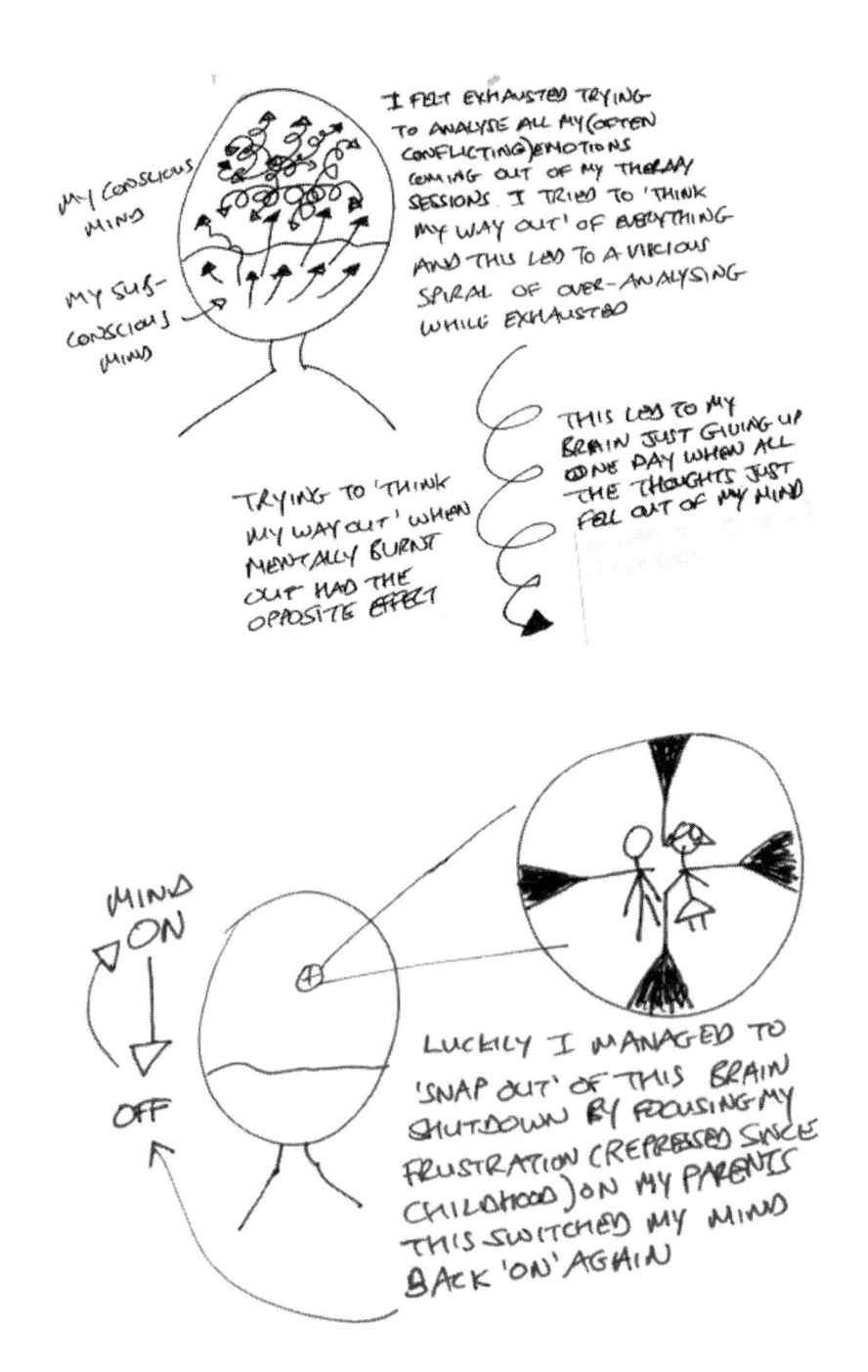

My conscious mind

My sub-conscious mind

I felt exhausted trying to analyse all my (often conflicting) emotions coming out of my therapy sessions. I tried to 'think my way out' of everything and this led to a vicious spiral of over-analysing while exhausted

Trying to 'think my way out' when mentally burnt out had the opposite effect

This led to my brain just giving up one day when all the thoughts just fell out of my mind

Mind ON → OFF

Luckily I managed to 'snap out' of this brain shutdown by focusing my frustration (repressed since childhood) on my parents. This switched my mind back 'on' again

SAVING YOURSELF   129

WHENEVER I FELT VERY FRUSTRATED, ANGRY, FED UP AND/OR CONFUSED I WOULD THINK ABOUT THE MAIN SOURCE OF MY REPRESSED EMOTIONS

MY PARENTS... AND FOCUS MY ENERGY ON IDENTIFYING AND OVERCOMING MY REMAINING UNADDRESSED FEARS AND INSECURITIES

FOCUSING ON THE SOURCE OF YOUR PROBLEMS ENSURES NO-ONE ELSE IN YOUR LIFE IS UNFAIRLY 'TARGETED' BY YOU...

'TARGETS' — ILLEGITIMATE (IN MY CASE)

PARTNER + KIDS

SIBLINGS

FRIENDS

TARGETING UNDERWAY

LIFE IN GENERAL

WORK COLLEAGUES

RANDOM PEOPLE

AVOIDING 'COLLATERAL' DAMAGE

My road to recovery looked like this.

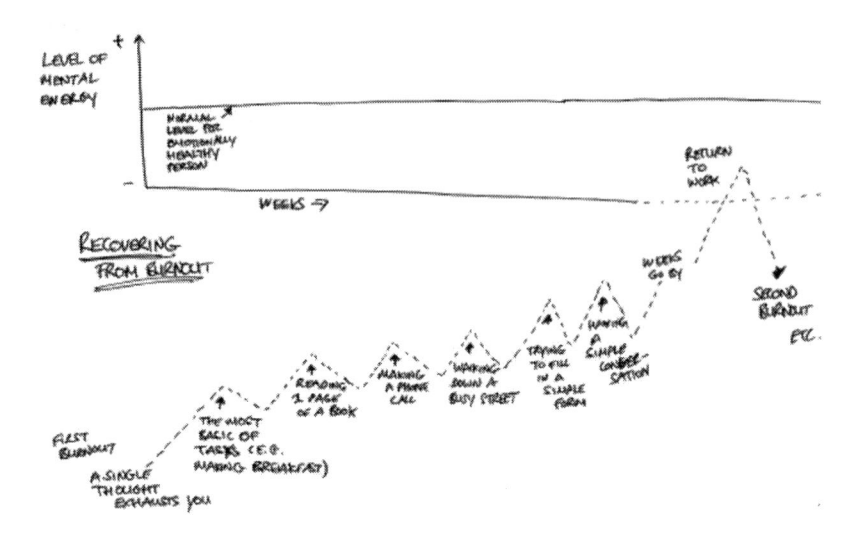

[Chart: "Recovering from Burnout" — showing level of mental energy over weeks, starting from "First Burnout — a single thought exhausts you", progressing through "The most basic of tasks (e.g. making breakfast)", "Reading 1 page of a book", "Making a phone call", "Walking down a busy street", "Trying to fill in a simple form", "Walking a simple conversation", up to "Return to work", then "Second Burnout etc."]

If you are determined to battle through it, you will come out at the other end with hugely improved self-respect and a much wiser outlook on life.

This chart compares 'normal' levels of emotional pain and fatigue to what you may experience.

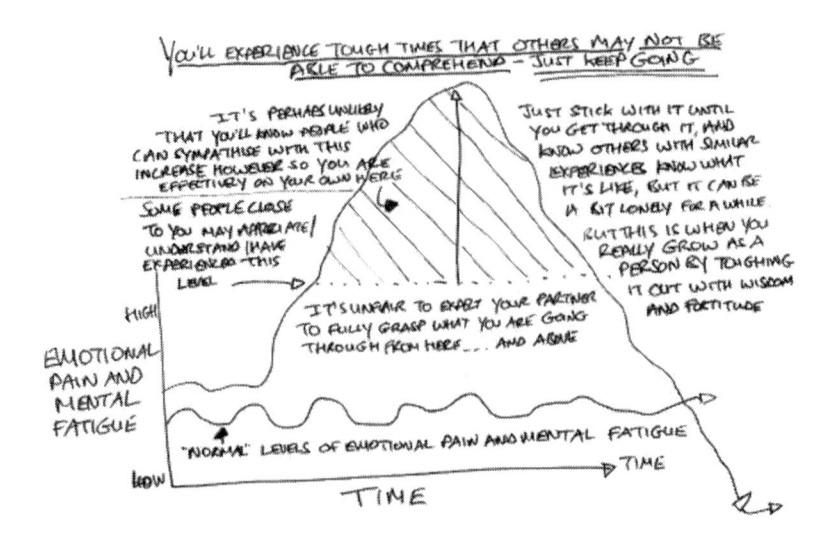

[Chart: Emotional pain and mental fatigue vs time, showing a large mountain shape above the "normal" level. Annotations: "You'll experience tough times that others may not be able to comprehend — just keep going"; "It's perhaps unlikely that you'll know people who can sympathise with this increase however so you are effectively on your own here"; "Some people close to you may appreciate / understand / have experienced this level"; "It's unfair to expect your partner to fully grasp what you are going through from here... and above"; "Just stick with it until you get through it, and know others with similar experiences know what it's like, but it can be a bit lonely for a while"; "But this is when you really grow as a person by toughing it out with wisdom and fortitude"]

ALCOHOL – SO VERY TEMPTING

When you are burnt out alcohol is very tempting because it gives you relief for a few hours from feeling fed up and exhausted. However, I relied on it for too long and it ended up causing me big problems – as I'm sure it has with a significant percentage of us. The only solution was a total time out from life in general staying in a special clinic for addiction problems. (See also an interesting article at www.vanschneider.com/no-alcohol-no-coffee-for-15-months-this-is-what-happened/)

I never thought I would give up alcohol. I never saw how this could ever be possible. And anyway, why would I? I used to think that everybody else drinks a bit too much and they seem to be fine, and I'm only doing it to help me relax and enjoy myself, and anyway, life is too short – dying with a healthy liver seems such a waste.

This was very much my mentality before going into therapy; very much a British/Irish thing perhaps (I'm part British and part Irish). All my friends got drunk at parties, weddings, stag weekends, at the races etc, so how can it be that bad? They all hold down good jobs, have healthy families seemingly, and seem to function well. And anyway, if I made sure it didn't affect me the next day (too much) then where was the harm?

The trouble with alcohol, as my father often told me, is that it is a good servant but a very bad master. It's fine when you are happy, but it's the devil when you are down and depressed – as I found out. It can lift the spirits when you are up, but it also dampens them when you are down. It encourages sociability when feeling open, and drives anti-social behaviour when you are feeling closed and frustrated.

I never thought in my wildest dreams that I would become critical of our drinking culture. Alcohol was the fuel for so many great nights in university and beyond. It gave me confidence and relaxed me when I needed it and it helped me to forget. However, once you've really considered the question of alcohol, in the cold light of day, from a sober perspective, it is remarkable the hold it has on our society. Recently, I did something that I never thought possible. I went to a best friend's fiftieth birthday party in a grand stately home with free booze all night – and I'm talking the best beers, champagne, wine, waiter service, free bar, good music, dancing, great event, reunion of old friends, great chat, no kids, lovely surroundings, free accommodation, a leisurely Sunday the next day – and I drank no alcohol the entire night. And I really enjoyed the occasion. Admittedly I went to bed shortly after midnight, but I don't think I missed much. Even better, nobody seemed to notice. I was paranoid that people would call me a party pooper, that I would not be able to follow drunken conversations, that I would feel left out of the fun, that I would be letting my friend down for not being there until the very end of the night … but nothing of the sort! The next day I woke up refreshed after a good night's sleep and I could remember everything about the night, all the conversations I had and with whom. What a revelation!

I managed this by first realising that my desire for alcohol was mixed up with my low sense of self-esteem and my desperate desire to be liked and accepted by other people. I drank to give myself the confidence to mingle and chat in social situations, because others were doing it and I wanted to fit in. I was desperately afraid of not being funny and engaging (which I subconsciously assumed people demanded of me). I subsequently drank to take away emotional and psychological pain. Once this latter reason had been addressed by taking a time out from life, I thought how rather pathetic it was of me to damage myself to please others.

I imagined myself going to this fiftieth birthday party and saying in my mind, 'Screw them, I'm going to show myself and them that I am not a social slave to alcohol'. With this determination to be independent and think for myself, the stage was set for my first big test. I have since been to a big weekend reunion of university friends which was a very boozy affair and managed not to drink at all then also. The feeling of pride and renewed self-esteem afterwards was great.

How did I reach this epiphany?

I had always really enjoyed a few pints. About the time I realised I needed help and sought therapy, I was drinking two or three times a week, up to five beers a session, not too much in the context of normal life I guess. As I got into therapy, I started drinking on my own much more often, and more regularly. (In general, I personally see nothing wrong with drinking on one's own occasionally when one is healthy; some of the nicest moments of personal reflection come with a quiet drink watching the world go by.)

As mentioned elsewhere, digging up and facing down one's innermost fears takes time and a lot of energy. Couple this with the ongoing insecurity, family life with young kids, and a professional job, and things quickly start getting demanding and fatigue starts setting in. Fatigue quickly leads to early-stage burnout and with that comes an unwillingness to socialise and a desire to escape the sense of crushing fatigue by lifting one's spirits momentarily with alcohol – a brief mental holiday. I also found out that sitting quietly on my own after one beer helped me to open up to myself about my fears and insecurities. This normally happened after a pint or two, up until the fourth or so, after which too much alcohol distorted my thinking too much.

I'm sure the professionals will have a go at me for saying this, but I genuinely could not have survived those long dark periods in the middle of therapy without alcohol. I had two young children, a job which demanded concentration and attention, and the other normal trappings of life. This period was quite productive for me in terms of therapy. It gave me the time to reflect on my own (and I would always make notes of what was going through my mind on the backs of beer mats etc.), to connect with my feelings, and the confidence to consider otherwise rather unpleasant truths about my life.

This was all right for the first year or two, but then the drinks became more numerous. I would drink ten pints of strong Continental beer without much food, but would be OK in the morning. I then started getting very aggressive when drunk, upsetting my poor wife on a few occasions (including one awful New Year's Eve when I woke up in an empty Irish pub at four in the morning not knowing what I had been doing), as well as some close friends. Luckily my wife pushed me to see a psychiatrist who was an expert in alcoholism.

I reluctantly went along and after a couple of sessions he suggested I have an intervention and come and stay in a special clinic for alcohol-dependent people. I almost laughed at the idea to begin with, believing I was not a drunk, saying to myself it was a cultural thing, this is what lots of people like me do socially. But after a few more drunken episodes I came to the realisation that maybe I was being excessive and, in part to placate my wife, called the psychiatrist and agreed to go to his clinic.

A few days later I arrived at a place that was a cross between a hospital and an old people's home. I remained there for over a month, only leaving on the weekends (with permission, and with an alcohol test on return).

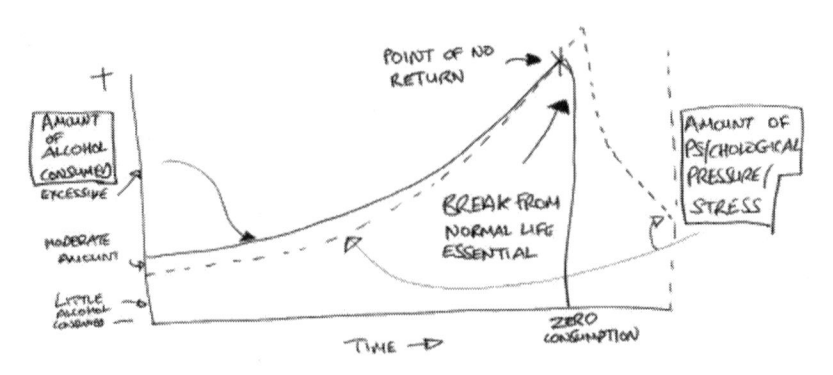

CORRELATION BETWEEN LEVELS OF STRESS AND ALCOHOL CONSUMPTION

MY TIME IN A RECOVERY CLINIC

This proved to be exactly what I needed – a complete break from life. I realised that the alcohol abuse was a symptom of the situation I was in, the cause of which was burnout with a degree of depression, a situation I could only manage if I could self-medicate every now and then using alcohol as if it were medicine, which was actually exacerbating the problem, weakening my health and scaring away my family.

It was a revelation waking up in the morning with absolutely nothing to do apart from turn up to breakfast, lunch and dinner, and attend the odd talking session with others in the clinic (with medical specialists). This total break from life gave me the time, the thinking space, the rest and the recuperation to move on in life. I am now very careful not to push myself so hard that the only way I can cope is to drink alcohol. I have simplified my life greatly since then, which helps a lot.

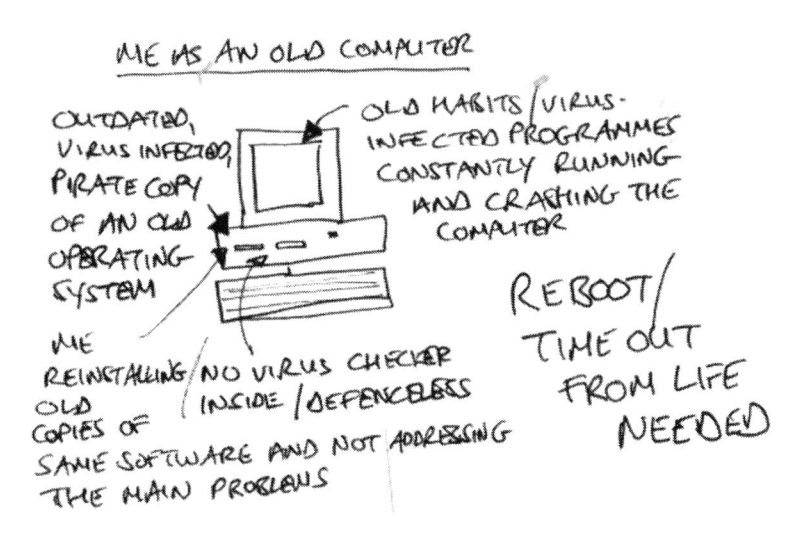

ME AS AN OLD COMPUTER

- OUTDATED, VIRUS INFECTED, PIRATE COPY OF AN OLD OPERATING SYSTEM
- OLD HABITS / VIRUS-INFECTED PROGRAMMES CONSTANTLY RUNNING AND CRASHING THE COMPUTER
- ME REINSTALLING / NO VIRUS CHECKER INSIDE / DEFENCELESS OLD COPIES OF SAME SOFTWARE AND NOT ADDRESSING THE MAIN PROBLEMS
- REBOOT / TIME OUT FROM LIFE NEEDED

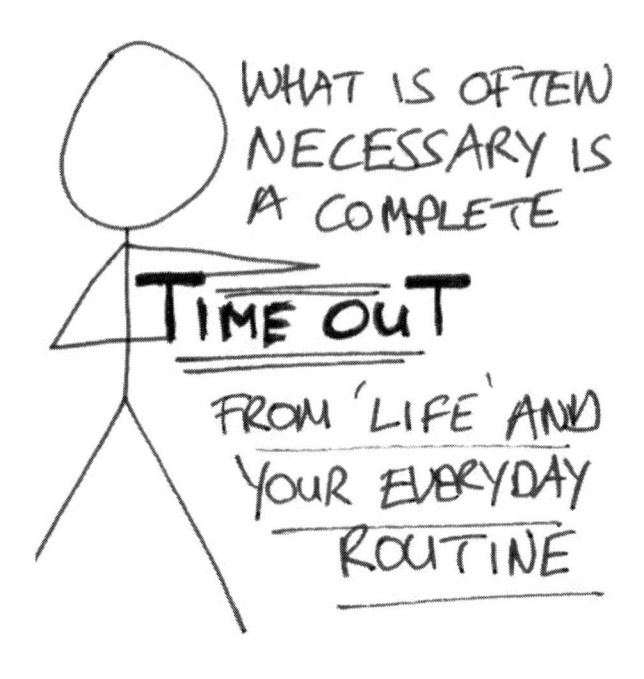

> **WHAT IS OFTEN NECESSARY IS A COMPLETE TIME OUT FROM 'LIFE' AND YOUR EVERYDAY ROUTINE**

The benefits from not drinking alcohol, at least for a while, are of course numerous. I remember how astonished I was to wake up on a Sunday morning and find myself feeling refreshed and full of energy, rather than slightly groggy, tired and a bit hungover from the night before. After a while, you suddenly seem to have so much more time on your hands. I now wake up early on a Saturday or Sunday morning, after having met a couple of friends the night before, and I've done all my chores before 9am, which still amazes me.

As a last remark on the subject, I wonder how many of us could go to a wedding without having a drink. I certainly could not have done so before my time out from life? How many would go to a wedding if it was clear that no alcohol would be available? Doesn't this show a level of habitual or social addiction? If so, should we be concerned. What does it say about our confidence and strength of character that we are reluctant to socialise with other nice people without the shield of alcohol? Just a few questions to ponder!

SAVING YOURSELF   137

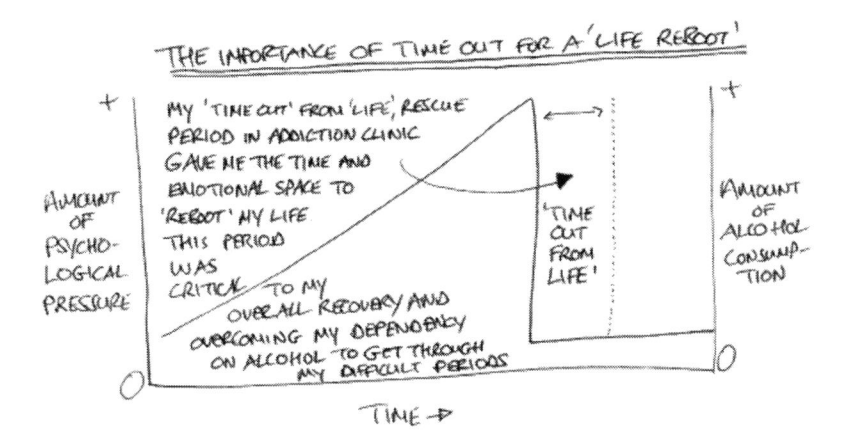

THE IMPORTANCE OF TIME OUT FOR A 'LIFE REBOOT'

MY 'TIME OUT' FROM 'LIFE', RESCUE PERIOD IN ADDICTION CLINIC GAVE ME THE TIME AND EMOTIONAL SPACE TO 'REBOOT' MY LIFE THIS PERIOD WAS CRITICAL TO MY OVERALL RECOVERY AND OVERCOMING MY DEPENDENCY ON ALCOHOL TO GET THROUGH MY DIFFICULT PERIODS

'TIME OUT FROM LIFE'

AMOUNT OF PSYCHOLOGICAL PRESSURE

AMOUNT OF ALCOHOL CONSUMPTION

TIME →

MANAGING YOUR RECOVERY PROCESS

I found the most useful procedure to follow during my 'journey' was something I have come to name as: Talk, Reflect, Draw, and Repeat. If such a procedure can be accompanied with a degree of resilience, then you will always be on the right road to full recovery.

TALK — ME / MY OLD THERAPIST

TALK: Have regular sessions talking to a professional therapist as honestly and as thoroughly as you can, for as long as you feel you need to. The goal is to release all your pent-up fears, insecurities and uncomfortable and intrusive thoughts. The only way to do so from my experience is to talk regularly with a qualified professional you feel comfortable with.

REFLECT — Hmm...?

REFLECT: Make notes after each therapy session about what goes through your mind between these sessions, or after you have completed a course of sessions. I still make time regularly to write down how I'm feeling, especially, for example, if I sense a new angle on a previous experience or I have an interesting dream. Seeing your thoughts and feelings written down in black and white is a terrific way to give them authenticity and legitimacy. Previously, I would have disregarded my thoughts as unpleasant intrusions, as dangerous and threatening things to be ignored. This is no cure of course, as they will just keep reappearing until you attend to them and give them the sense of legitimacy they crave (the uncomfortable emotions within you want to be given a voice). One way of doing this is by putting them down on paper which crystallises and manifests your thinking process.

DRAW: Once you have a certain amount of notes covering assorted topics (and you will no doubt unearth many issues worth pondering), revisit them occasionally and reflect on them. You may have days when nothing comes to mind, but I found I more often had days when I just didn't have enough time to process everything flying around in my mind that deserved attention. When the latter occurs, find a quiet space (or ideally go for a long walk) and try to conceptualise what you are thinking and feeling into some form of images. Drawings can reflect and illuminate the feelings, memories, realisations and revelations about your past. Drawing them out helped me hugely to understand what was going on in the depths of my mind, where the fears and insecurities tend to lurk. To being with, it was a bit tricky, but the more you talk and the more you build up a body of notes to reflect upon the easier it becomes to conceptualise and draw your emotions. Seeing your thoughts and feelings written down is great, as mentioned above, but drawing them out gives them much more life, vitality, meaning and context, enabling you to understand yourself so much better. (As you well know, the brain thinks in images rather than text – "a picture paints a thousand words" and all that.)

REPEAT

REPEAT: Keep going until you feel you have done enough and revisit whenever you feel the need.

The added beauty of this approach is that you can convey to your partner, close friends or close family members (as well as yourself, of course) much more precisely what you are feeling, and perhaps why, which goes a long way to relieving them of their possible anxiety about what you are going through. I found that this becomes a virtuous circle as it led to my wife feeling included and in the loop to some extent during what can be a trying time for the both of you.

The importance of resilience: It is worth reminding ourselves that the Talk, Reflect, Draw, Repeat process will take time. Completing any form of emotional process requires tenacity, commitment, energy and more importantly, resilience. There is an excellent short book on the topic of resilience in the Harvard Business Review series *Emotional Intelligence*. The book lists the following responses as crucial to the development of resilience.

A staunch acceptance of reality: This is fundamental to overcoming our deeply engrained insecurities and fears. Without an acceptance of reality, it is very easy to "slip into denial as a coping mechanism" as the Harvard *Emotional Intelligence* series states: denial that we have fears and insecurities and that there is anything wrong with us, denial that they are affecting us in anyway and denial that they need to be confronted and overcome.

Comforting untruths are a form of intellectual dishonesty. It's much better to face up to the sometimes-harsh reality with dignity and self-respect.

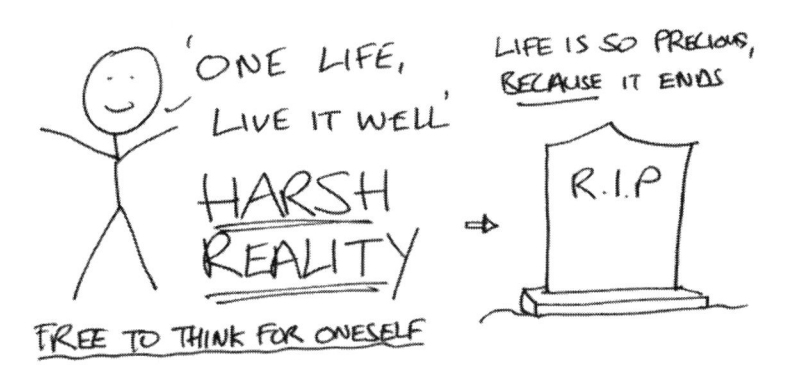

I found myself attempting to do this after I had thought very carefully, and read very widely, about the truthfulness of my religious beliefs. After concluding that I had become an atheist, I had to face the stark reality that I now believed I would not have an eternal life after death with all my loved ones, as taught to me since childhood, but rather, once my life is over, I will be gone for all eternity, never to be ever again. Because I had never questioned this concept of an afterlife, and having believed it without question for so long, this was a rather wrenching realisation that struck me very hard for some time.

I found myself for some time afterwards feeling rather frightened and bewildered by this jarring epiphany. However, I was able to slowly come to terms with this new reality (and I have since regarded life as much more precious as a result) and I now feel more robust as a person.

Another example was when I tried to confront some deep fears which felt especially disturbing. As I forced myself to try and confront them, I would suddenly find myself in my imagination in an empty, arid rocky desert expecting to be attacked by demons. After holding my ground in my imagination for a bit, I felt a very warm wind whistling directly past me as if the fears were trying to make a rather forlorn attempt to scare me. This image often reappeared to me when I subsequently tried to confront other fears I had – such as realising that I was in a Damien Lewis *Band of Brothers* moment, with two German positions either side of us, and his group about to be discovered...

A deep belief that life is meaningful: I found this very much to be true as it can give you a greater motivation to continue the sometimes seemingly fruitless process of saving yourself from your fears. The Harvard Business Review volume entitled Resilience also mentions the usefulness of having a strong value system. Sound ethical and moral principles, which infuse your personal environment, provide meaning to your existence. The book cites the amazing example of Viktor E. Frankl's experiences in Auschwitz, which he recounted in *Man's Search for Meaning*. During his time in the death camp Frankl found that the only way to carry on was to focus on a meaningful goal to be achieved in the future, in his case imagining giving lectures after the end of the war on the psychology of the prison camp to convey to others what he had been through. The focus on a positive goal, despite not knowing if he would live, was crucial to Frankl's psychological survival.

A universe away, in my little world, I tried to educate myself on certain topics when I was in my deepest hole, for instance learning as much as I could about personal investing and entrepreneurship – skills that I thought would help me in the future. This focus on positive topics for future benefit helped maintain my spirits when I was otherwise feeling truly rock bottom about my self-value and self-esteem. I also slowly realised that emotional pain is directly proportional to emotional growth. The more painful it is to overcome your fears and insecurities, the more you grow as a person and respect yourself, which is vital currency for people like us.

A great ability to improvise: The ability to 'bounce back' and improvise in whatever situation one finds oneself. I guess I could argue that my writing this book could qualify as a way of 'bouncing back' from the hole I was in (but perhaps that's for others to judge).

The Harvard Business Review volume on resilience also mentions the importance of "possession of an inner psychological space" as protection from abuse. I recall that Tiger Woods's father gave him advice, just before he won the US Masters golf open at an amazingly young age, which went something like, "Just get into your own little world Tiger and just smash them". Which he went on to do, of course. This notion of being able to find a place of refuge and safety in your own mind where you can plan your recovery in a calm and private manner seems critical to me.

Other characteristics referred to in the Harvard book are a sense of curiosity and a good sense of humour (often black) where you can laugh at the often preposterous psychological mindsets we no doubt often find (or found) ourselves in.

IMPROVING THE WAY YOU THINK – MENTAL MODELS

Much of saving yourself from childhood trauma, and the resulting effects on your adult life, can be addressed by improving the way you think.

Use mental models to strip away your insecurities and fears, which are often based on false assumptions and misreading of others' intentions. A child has an egocentric view of the world. If something bad happens, the child assumes they must be at fault. This view is backed up by cognitive bias, which Wikipedia defines as the "tendency to search for, interpret, favour, and recall information in a way that confirms one's pre-existing beliefs or hypotheses… The effect is stronger for emotionally charged issues and for deeply entrenched beliefs."

In an excellent article titled *Mental Models I Find Repeatedly Useful*, Gabriel Weinberg offers examples of models that can help us understand our perceptions of reality in a more informed manner. (https://medium.com/@yegg/mental-models-i-find-repeatedly-useful-936f1cc405d)

- **Hanlon's Razor**— "Never attribute to malice that which is adequately explained by carelessness." (Related: fundamental attribution error—"the tendency for people to place an undue emphasis on internal characteristics of the agent (character or intention), rather than external factors, in explaining another person's behaviour in a given situation.")
- **Occam's Razor**— "Among competing hypotheses, the one with the fewest assumptions should be selected." (Related: conjunction fallacy, overfitting, "when you hear hoofbeats, think of horses not zebras.")
- **Cognitive Biases**— "Tendencies to think in certain ways that can lead to systematic deviations from a standard of rationality or good judgments."

- **Arguing from First Principles**—"A first principle is a basic, foundational, self-evident proposition or assumption that cannot be deduced from any other proposition or assumption." From this I deduced that virtually all parents love their children.
- **Proximate vs Root Cause**— "A proximate cause is an event which is closest to, or immediately responsible for causing, some observed result. This exists in contrast to a higher-level ultimate cause (or distal cause) which is usually thought of as the 'real' reason something occurred." (Related: 5 whys—"to determine the root cause of a defect or problem by repeating the question 'Why?') From this I deduced that the proximate cause is that my parents are the reason I suffered; but the root cause is their trauma from childhood, so they can't be blamed too much for their actions.
- **Thought Experiment**— 'Considers some hypothesis, theory, or principle for the purpose of thinking through its consequences." (Related: counterfactual thinking) From this I thought, imagine your parents at your funeral, they would be utterly and overwhelmingly devastated.
- **Systems Thinking**—"By taking the overall system as well as its parts into account systems thinking is designed to avoid potentially contributing to further development of unintended consequences." (Related: "Can't see the forest for the trees.") From this I observed how my father acted in different social settings. I noticed how uncomfortable he was with close relatives, suggesting some form of suffering from childhood shame. This new perspective of him, in a wider setting, really softened my view of him.
- **Power-Law**—"A functional relationship between two quantities, where a relative change in one quantity results in a proportional relative change in the other quantity, independent of the initial size of those quantities: one quantity varies as a power of another." Shaming a child is a good example of this; a small amount of shaming a child

can lead to associated massive increases in self-doubt and self-loathing.
- **Catalyst**—"A substance which increases the rate of a chemical reaction." (Related: tipping point.) From this I see that reminders of your childhood experiences (social situations, people from your past etc.) can easily tip you into a child ego state where you re-experience childhood fears and insecurities.
- **IQ vs EQ**—"IQ is a total score derived from one of several standardized tests designed to assess human intelligence." "EQ is the capacity of individuals to recognize their own, and other people's emotions, to discriminate between different feelings and label them appropriately, and to use emotional information to guide thinking and behaviour." I recognise this as one of the great benefits of self-driven emotional recovery from negative mindsets.
- **Growth Mindset vs Fixed Mindset**—"Those with a 'fixed mindset' believe that abilities are mostly innate and interpret failure as the lack of necessary basic abilities, while those with a 'growth mindset' believe that they can acquire any given ability provided they invest effort or study." A growth mindset is critical to have if you want to fully recover from emotional trauma.
- **Nature vs Nurture**—"The relative importance of an individual's innate qualities as compared to an individual's personal experiences in causing individual differences, especially in behavioural traits." If you have experienced emotional trauma, nearly all the evidence seems to point to nurture rather than nature in this respect. It's not you, it's what happened to you.

THE POWER OF IMAGINATION – UTILISE IT TO THE FULL!

To relax in the evenings, I would lie in my hammock and imagine what I would most like to be doing at that time to alleviate feelings of burnout and a sense of frustration. I would then choose to listen to music that matched my mood.

WHERE DO I WANT TO GO IN MY IMAGINATION THIS EVENING?

THIS COULD BE IMAGINING MYSELF GOING CRAZY IN A TECHNO CLUB IN BERLIN

OR HEADBANGING TO THRASH METAL IN SEATTLE

OR MEDITATING NEAR A CLEAR BLUE CLEAN ON A BEAUTIFUL BEACH

[Sketch: two stick figures in a boxing ring, labelled "OR BEATING SOMEBODY UP IN A KICK-BOXING RING"]

Another topic I found helpful was the philosophical subject of existentialism. This sounds rather grand but it seems to be relatively simple. You are free to define your own purpose in life and there is no pre-defined purpose handed down to you from on-high. This is encapsulated by the phrase 'existence comes before essence', which means you come into existence first and then you define the essence of your life. This to me was a really liberating concept. Rather than feeling submissive to the will of others and to God I suddenly realised I can define my own essence of life – what the purpose of life is, how I wish to lead it and hence take responsibility and enjoy the rewards of all my own decisions. Some regard existentialism as somewhat frightening as you have to define life's purpose for yourself, and you alone are responsible for all your actions. I take the opposite view: that this freedom is liberating rather than something to be feared.

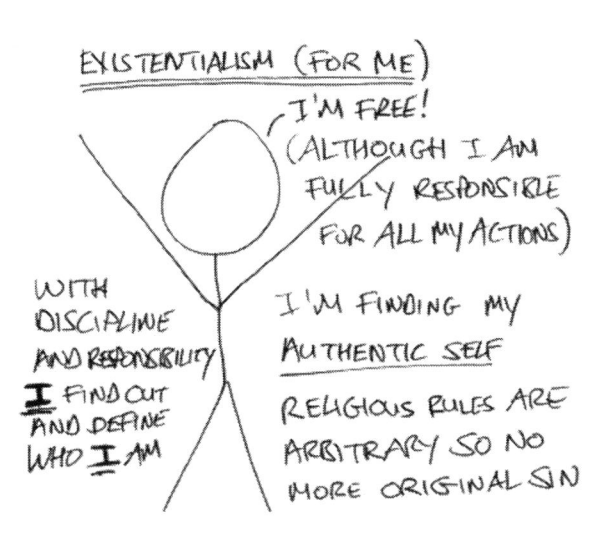

[Sketch: stick figure with arms raised, labelled:]

EXISTENTIALISM (FOR ME)

- I'M FREE! (ALTHOUGH I AM FULLY RESPONSIBLE FOR ALL MY ACTIONS)
- WITH DISCIPLINE AND RESPONSIBILITY I FIND OUT AND DEFINE WHO I AM
- I'M FINDING MY AUTHENTIC SELF
- RELIGIOUS RULES ARE ARBITRARY SO NO MORE ORIGINAL SIN

A Martin Luther King Jr. speech to a group of school leavers included some very memorable recommendations for life.

> SPEECH BY MARTIN LUTHER KING Jr.
>
> 'YOUR LIFE'S BLUEPRINT'
>
> "... A DEEP BELIEF IN YOUR OWN DIGNITY, YOUR WORTH, AND YOUR OWN SOMEBODINESS. DON'T ALLOW ANYBODY TO MAKE YOU FEEL THAT YOU'RE NOBODY. ALWAYS FEEL THAT YOU COUNT. ALWAYS FEEL THAT YOU HAVE WORTH, AND ALWAYS FEEL THAT YOUR LIFE HAS ULTIMATE SIGNIFICANCE..."
>
> PHILADELPHIA, OCTOBER 1967

MANAGING THE PROCESS – SOME MORE TIPS

Feel your emotions; don't be ashamed of having them – they just 'are'. There are no good or bad emotions. Remember, you feel them for a reason. In fact, rejoice in the fact that you have found them (it's what makes us all human). Have the courage to feel your emotions, own them (they are you, after all), rationalise them, put them into perspective and let out all of that trapped steam.

You may feel that some of your true feelings just don't want to be uncovered. It's a weird feeling, as you may find yourself connecting with parts of yourself, your memories, your fears, that you didn't know you had and that don't really feel fully part of you as you know yourself on that day. When that happened to me, I saw it as a sign that I was making real progress.

I often felt I had connected with a part of me that had been totally forgotten about, like a small me in a small locked room somewhere in my soul or subconscious, or gut, and I felt a slight elation when this part of me had been found again.

Imagine yourself as a child in a room on its own. What would the grown you say to it?

Beware of jumping from insecurity to arrogance, without going through the steps in between. If you feel yourself overanalysing then stop, and do something else.

It's a long journey from small scared child to confident, wise, mature adult. A long but hugely rewarding journey. Embarking on this journey is a bit like driving a car. You need to make lots of small corrections to make sure you stay in the right lane and proceed at the right speed.

Channel your anger into something positive, like a renewed determination to overcome your fears and insecurities, for example by writing them all down. Otherwise, anger is just a waste of time and energy.

Try to understand why certain people acted the way they did. If your father never gave you any attention, perhaps it was because he too had a difficult upbringing. Don't start allocating blame for your state of mind. Whatever you say in anger can be deeply damaging. Life is too short, accept it with magnanimity and move on – it will be good for you/for your self-respect and won't cause lasting offence/hurt.

At some point each week, or even each day, you will feel slightly better, slightly more unified, confident and 'together'. This means you are on the right path. Now it's just a question of keeping going, one step after another. Each day will bring a new positive realisation which you can use to motivate yourself for the next day.

Talk to your partner about any therapy sessions you are doing, if you feel comfortable about doing so – they'll probably be very concerned and will appreciate the updates. It's also good for you and for the relationship. They will be supporting you, so keep them in the loop.

Get in the zone – where your mind is clear, you are comfortable, there are no distractions and let your mind wander, gently guiding it, redirecting it where and when necessary, but not so much as this becomes a distraction. Stay in the zone as much as you can and let your subconscious throw things up into your conscious, then let these thoughts develop gently – don't pull at them, jump on them or smother them. Let them grow by themselves with some nurturing

Don't fight it, feel it. When negative thoughts reappear again, confront them if they are fears. Towards the end of the process, feel them and let them happen – you won't fear them anymore – then analyse them from a distance.

You will feel a sense of achievement and pride when you face and overcome your fears, one by one, bit by bit. Imagine the fear as some form of ghost train ghoul dangling in front of you in the way. Now imagine yourself walking towards this ghoul and straight through it with the realisation that it can't hurt you and that it's harmless. (As I imagined myself in the desert feeling a warm wind building up and swooping towards me with an evil face/figure at the front. I didn't move a muscle as it blew over and past me and faded away in the distance.)

Once you bring these childlike emotions into the daylight and accept them as yours, you can become, in some ways, proud of them, or at least not ashamed of them. Once you are open about them to yourself and your friends and family, then they gently disperse. Your acceptance of these as your legitimate feelings removes the fear of having them. Once the fear is gone, they dissipate, because you are no longer focused on contending with them.

Learn to rise above your thoughts. View them as if you were a bird flying over them. Learn to separate your instinctive reactions/fears/negative thoughts from your analysis of them.

It's a cliché but it's also true: real beauty comes from within.

Balance is important. Treat your recovery process with a healthy dose of humour and emotional distance. Yes, you are probably a victim of some sort, but you also probably have a huge amount to be thankful for, as you will see.

Appreciate the tough times. Your character will be revealed, and you will achieve real insight into your problems.

Remind yourself that other people have suffered much more. It was a whole lot worse being in the trenches in the First World War. Be magnanimous and forgiving. Understand why other people acted in a certain way and try to take an enlightened approach. Put your suffering into perspective – I would not like to take my share of the world's suffering!

If you have a thought, try and hold it gently in your mind, go to a quiet place, and let it gently develop and then take its reins and lead it.

Realise your therapist and/or psychiatrist have your best interests at heart. Think about topics, dreams, issues that you would like to raise with your therapist prior to each session, to get the most out of it.

Make brief notes after each therapy session. It's amazing how much you may discuss and it's always useful to glance over these again at a later date to remind yourself of certain realisations you experienced. It helps to solidify the progress made and makes it easier the next time you revisit a certain topic.

No matter how hard they try, it's unlikely your partner can appreciate your struggle. Nor should they be expected to. It can therefore be a rather lonely and frustrating process. You may have to swallow a lot of well-meant but inconsiderate remarks such as, "You are always so tired" and "Why can't you make more of an effort with my friends?". You'll just have to take these on the chin and direct your frustration into getting better.

Without wanting to put anyone off, it's a very tough daily struggle from an unbelievably low base, just to get back to some level of normality. It's something that most people will never get near to understanding, nor should they have to. Just remember, those days of emotional pain lead to emotional growth. Just as your muscles may hurt after a session at the gym, then so will you after a session making great progress in finding your way out of your deep emotional hole. That's why it's great talking to other people who have suffered similar abuse and who are working their way through it (although be wary of those who haven't reached your level of recovery as they may just drag you back – you have to be pretty selfish at this stage of your life).

Kids are an added pressure, but they can also be very helpful in helping you to find and reconnect with your wounded inner child.

Marry well!! Luckily, I married a lovely, emotionally stable woman. Dickstein et al. (2004) suggest that the presence and active participation of a secure and adaptively functioning partner/spouse may serve to offset the effects of negative childhood relational experiences.

Stay healthy. Long walks and jogging are great for self-reflection. Gym sessions help to beat those body blues. Mountain biking in nature is great, as is swimming, and of course, lots of healthy food, rest and sleep. Going for long walks or running whenever possible is a terrific way to collect your thoughts and work out where you are. Meditation, mindfulness, weight training, running, sleep, and breathing practices are all helpful.

Find your inner voice and practice using it until it's strong and loud. There's no point being a small you. Once you're free, then focus on ideas, lofty ideas in life.

Imagine a list of great human attributes, and you coming very high up on the list. If I were somebody else and noticed me walk past, I would think, wow, what a tall, kind-looking attractive man.

Always visualise a way out when in despair. There are always ways out.

CONCLUSION

I will leave the last word on the topic of ensuring mental health to Donald Winnicott, a British paediatrician and psychoanalyst (7 April 1896 – 25 January 1971). I saw a fascinating video by the School of Life on YouTube titled *Psychotherapy – Donald Winnicott* highlighting how he regarded one of the most important ways to improve human well-being was a rather simple one: better raising of children by their parents, and being 'good enough parents'. He proposed the following. While some of this line of argument perhaps needs updating, his general message seems to me both simple, 'cost effective' and eminently plausible.

- Your child is very vulnerable, so adults should adapt and not impose their needs on it.
- Allow the child to cry in a state of rage, often because of fear. Be calm so the child realises he has nothing to fear.
- Beware of 'good children' before their time, as they have a false self, because adults have demanded too much compliance from them at an early age.
- Let your child be, empathise.
- Realise how important parenting is, a parent is as important as the prime minister, the factory for the next set of well-rounded empathic citizens. LOVE! Surrender one's own ego for close and attentive listening to a mystery unwrapping itself – a child – and keep calm.

In short, perhaps our society needs to focus more on being even better at parenting, by understanding more and adapting to a child's needs to ensure they are properly loved, so that books like these, for whatever they are worth, are no longer needed!

APPENDICES

I thought I would add, for gentle consideration and reflection, the great British philosopher Bertrand Russell's version of the ten commandments.

1. Do not feel absolutely certain of anything.
2. Do not think it worthwhile to produce belief by concealing evidence, for the evidence is sure to come to light.
3. Never try to discourage thinking, for you are sure to succeed.
4. When you meet with opposition, even if it should be from your husband or your children, endeavour to overcome it by argument and not by authority, for a victory dependent upon authority is unreal and illusory.
5. Have no respect for the authority of others, for there are always contrary authorities to be found.
6. Do not use power to suppress opinions you think pernicious, for if you do the opinions will suppress you.
7. Do not fear to be eccentric in opinion, for every opinion now accepted was once eccentric.
8. Find more pleasure in intelligent dissent than in passive agreement, for, if you value intelligence as you should, the former implies a deeper agreement than the latter.
9. Be scrupulously truthful, even when truth is inconvenient, for it is more inconvenient when you try to conceal it.
10. Do not feel envious of the happiness of those who live in a fool's paradise, for only a fool will think that it is happiness.

In the same vein I also found Richard Dawkins' Alternative Ten Commandments useful as cited in his book *The God Delusion*:

1. Do not do to others what you would not want them to do to you.
2. In all things, strive to cause no harm.
3. Treat your fellow human beings, your fellow living things, and the world in general with love, honesty, faithfulness and respect.
4. Do not overlook evil or shrink from administering justice, but always be ready to forgive wrongdoing freely admitted and honestly regretted.
5. Live life with a sense of joy and wonder.
6. Always seek to be learning something new.
7. Test all things; always check your ideas against the facts, and be ready to discard even a cherished belief if it does not conform to them.
8. Never seek to censor or cut yourself off from dissent; always respect the right of others to disagree with you.
9. Form independent opinions based on your own reason and experience; do not allow yourself to be led blindly by others.
10. Question everything.

If you liked How to Sort your Head Out I would really appreciate you adding a quick review of it on your favourite sites (it shouldn't take more than a few minutes), and thanks in advance for considering this!

For more information on Luke and his work, please go to www.lukepemberton.com

A percentage of sales of this book will be donated to CALM
(Charity Reg No: 1110621, www.thecalmzone.net)

IN SUPPORT OF

CAMPAIGN
AGAINST
LIVING
MISERABLY

CALM

If you liked this book I would really appreciate you adding a quick review of it on your favourite sites (it shouldn't take more than a few minutes) and thanks in advance for considering this!

For more information on Luke and his work please go to www.lukepemberton.com

Printed in Poland
by Amazon Fulfillment
Poland Sp. z o.o., Wrocław